At Issue

Drunk Driving

Other Books in the At Issue Series:

At Issue

Drunk Driving

Stefan Kiesbye, Book Editor

GREENHAVEN PRESS
A part of Gale, Cengage Learning

Detroit • New York • San Francisco • New Haven, Conn • Waterville, Maine • London

GALE
CENGAGE Learning

Christine Nasso, *Publisher*
Elizabeth Des Chenes, *Managing Editor*

© 2011 Greenhaven Press, a part of Gale, Cengage Learning.

Gale and Greenhaven Press are registered trademarks used herein under license.

For more information, contact:
Greenhaven Press
27500 Drake Rd.
Farmington Hills, MI 48331-3535
Or you can visit our Internet site at gale.cengage.com

For product information and technology assistance, contact us at

Gale Customer Support, 1-800-877-4253
For permission to use material from this text or product, submit all requests online at www.cengage.com/permissions

Further permissions questions can be emailed to permissionrequest@cengage.com

Articles in Greenhaven Press anthologies are often edited for length to meet page requirements. In addition, original titles of these works are changed to clearly present the main thesis and to explicitly indicate the author's opinion. Every effort is made to ensure that Greenhaven Press accurately reflects the original intent of the authors. Every effort has been made to trace the owners of copyrighted material.

Cover Image copyright © Images.com/Corbis.

LIBRARY OF CONGRESS CATALOGING-IN-PUBLICATION DATA

Drunk driving / Stefan Kiesbye, book editor.
    p. cm. -- (At issue)
   Includes bibliographical references and index.
   ISBN 978-0-7377-5841-2 (hardcover) -- ISBN 978-0-7377-5842-9 (pbk.)
  1. Drunk driving--United States. 2. Drunk driving--United States--Prevention. I. Kiesbye, Stefan.
   HE5620.D72D785 2011
   363.12'5140973--dc22
                                                      2011008689

Printed in the United States of America
2 3 4 5 6   18 17 16 15 14

Contents

Introduction

Many adults have faced a dilemma after a dinner party at a friend's house, a birthday celebration at a restaurant, or a night out on the town: leave the car behind and call a cab, or drive home intoxicated, as carefully as possible. The failure to see the full measure of danger lurking in this situation convinces many drivers to take risks that could very well lead to disaster.

According to the Center for Disease Control and Prevention (CDC), "16,885 people in the U.S. died [in 2005] in alcohol-related motor vehicle crashes, representing 39% of all traffic-related deaths. . . . Nearly 1.4 million drivers were arrested for driving under the influence of alcohol or narcotics. . . . That's less than one percent of the 159 million self-reported episodes of alcohol-impaired driving among U.S. adults each year."

In December 2009, Connie Ann Strout drove, as reported by the *Minneapolis Star Tribune*, with a blood alcohol level of ".17 percent, more than twice the legal limit of 0.08 percent." Her car struck that of Tao Thao and his wife Yia Vang, who was pregnant with the couple's unborn son. The fetus was killed in the accident. Stroud later said, "I will spend my life thinking about what I did. . . . I feel your pain. I am so sorry."

In March 2008, the *Windsor Star*, Canada, wrote that student Whitney Camlis,

> Caught only a glimpse in her rearview mirror of the approaching van [. . .] "The next thing I remember is a woman had her hand through my driver-side window, because all my windows were shattered, and she was praying for me and with me," said the 20-year-old LaSalle [Ontario] woman, who suffered a concussion, cuts, collapsed lung, and four broken vertebrae.

Camlis was hit by a 71-year-old man driving under the influence. "Her 1991 Oldsmobile Cutlass, destroyed front and back, crashed into the van ahead of her. The van that hit her careened into a ditch."

Neither of the drunk drivers involved in these accidents had any malicious intent, but they did knowingly take what they must have initially viewed as an acceptable risk. That's the reason why many states—with penalties for impaired drivers that were negligible when compared to punishments for drug dealers, burglars, and fraudulent business people—have adopted tougher laws to prosecute drunk drivers, treating their actions as serious crimes and putting them behind bars.

But the question remains whether or not these new laws help deter drunk drivers, many of whom suffer from alcoholism. Professor David Hanson at the State University of New York, Potsdam, is convinced that prison sentences are of little use in solving the problem of drunk driving fatalities, as he writes on his website Alcohol Problems & Solutions. "Jail or prison sentences for alcohol offenses, in spite of their great popularity, appear to be of little value in deterring high BAC [blood alcohol content] drivers. In short, it appears that we can't 'jail our way out of the problem.'" He claims that the "perception of swift and certain punishment is more important than severity."

Instead of jailing offenders, Hanson makes a case for DWI (driving while impaired) courts, sometimes called DUI (driving under the influence) courts, sobriety courts, wellness courts, or accountability courts. He states that they have been effective in cutting down on drunk driving incidents. "Such courts address the problem of hard-core repeat offenders by treating alcohol addiction or alcoholism. The recidivism or failure rate of DWI courts is very low."

Huntington Beach, California may try a different route altogether. According to the *Los Angeles Times*, the city is considering a new tactic against drunk driving: public shaming on Facebook. After the idea was suggested Monday at a City Council meeting, the city's Police Department is looking into posting the names of suspected drunk drivers on Facebook, said Lt. Russell Reinhart. Councilman Devin Dwyer asked police if they could post the names of people arrested for drunk driving on the city's Facebook page, because the local newspaper has stopped publishing the listings. "I didn't think public shaming for driving under the influence was such a bad idea," Dwyer said. "I would use any tool necessary to bring down the numbers of drunk drivers."

It remains to be seen if stiffer penalties, DUI courts, or programs such as the Huntington Beach proposal can be successful. However, the first step every driver should take is to be aware of the very real and very serious consequences drunk driving can have. As Hanson writes, "volunteer to be a designated driver," and "don't ever let your friends drive drunk. Take their keys, have them stay the night, have them ride home with someone else, call a cab, or do whatever else is necessary—but don't let them drive!" The authors of the viewpoints in At Issue: Drunk Driving explore the impact drunk driving has on society as well as possible solutions to decrease devastating accidents and keep the roads safe.

1

New Laws Are Needed in the Fight Against Drunk and Reckless Drivers

David King and Gail Robinson

David King is the State Government Editor at the Gotham Gazette. *Gail Robinson is Editor-In-Chief of the* Gotham Gazette.

After recent highly publicized drunk driving accidents, New York state has responded by introducing new laws against offenders. While these are considered among the toughest nationwide, the legislature has done comparatively little to curb reckless driving, a problem that has not been in the public spotlight, but that is equally dangerous. To make streets and highways safer, legislators need to consider measures that effectively punish those who disregard the safety of pedestrians and other motorists. If New York wants to improve drivers' safety, it needs to address both drunk and reckless driving.

Even if they don't know Diane Schuler by name probably every sentient New Yorker knows what she did and the horror she created. On July 26, [2009] Schuler, apparently under the influence of vodka and marijuana, drove the wrong way on the Taconic Parkway, only stopping when her minivan collided with another vehicle, killing herself, her daughter, her three nieces and three people in the other car.

But what about Isaac Chehebar? In 2001, Chehebar raced his Porsche at twice the speed limit down Brooklyn's Ocean

David King and Gail Robinson, "Death by Car," *Gotham Gazette*, November 23, 2009. Reproduced by permission.

Parkway, colliding with two teenage sisters walking along that boulevard's median strip. He killed both of them and seriously injured their mother. Chehebar apparently was a reckless driver—but, at least in this instance, apparently a sober one.

Last week the New York State legislature, after some debate and disagreement, agreed to lake another move to crack down on drunk drivers, particularly those, like Schuler, who have children in their vehicles. The vote won widespread praise as one of the few worthwhile things the legislature has managed to accomplish this year.

The action continues what has been the practice in New York and much of the nation: getting tough on drunk drivers and the accidents they cause while doing little to combat the many death and injuries caused by people who, while unimpaired, still drive badly and even recklessly.

Leandra's Law

The bill passed by the legislature last week, Leandra's Law, makes it a felony for anyone to drive with a blood alcohol level of .08 or higher while transporting a child under age 15. It also requires interlocks in the vehicles of anyone convicted of driving while intoxicated in New York State. Interlocks periodically measure the blood alcohol content of the driver's breath and incapacitate the vehicle if the alcohol level is too high. Experts have estimated the devices could prevent between 35 and 65 percent of potential recurrences of drunk driving.

The new law is considered to be among the toughest on drunk driving in the country. Only one other state, Arizona, makes it a felony to drive under the influence with a minor in the car, and while over 40 states utilize interlocks, most of them require it only in extreme cases of multiple offenses or extremely high alcohol levels. California Gov. Arnold Schwarzenegger recently signed a bill mandating the use of interlocks for those convicted of driving while intoxicated.

A sense of pride and purpose seemed to sweep over legislators as supporters of the bill learned they would pass the legislation. Gov. David Paterson and legislators declared that the bill might not have been signed into law had it not been for Lenny Rosado, the father of Leandra, an 11-year-old girl who was killed when the car in which she was riding flipped on the Henry Hudson Parkway in Manhattan. The driver, the mother of one of her friends, apparently was under the influence of alcohol and marijuana.

Rosado said that, for a moment, he was overwhelmed by Albany. "I went home and said, 'Wow, politics! This is just insane!'" Rosado admitted moments after the Senate passed the bill. "But today, for these people to come together and all be on the same page and pass the bill was really something."

Chain of Tragedies

According to Assembly and Senate sources it look a perfect storm to allow the bill to make it into law. The storm started this summer with the Schuler tragedy.

In August [2009], Paterson and Republican Charles Fuschillo introduced nearly identical proposals to stiffen the punishment for those who drive under the influence of alcohol with minors in the car.

Drivers can use an alternative vehicle to avoid the interlock, and there are also privacy issues.

The death of Leandra Rosado followed in October [2009]. And Rosado started a petition drive to toughen the laws. Soon the *Daily News* and other papers were covering Rosado's every move. He even appeared on Oprah. But that was not enough to get the bill passed.

When the legislature returned this month [November 2009], the Assembly wanted to weaken the legislation by raising the blood alcohol level required for a felony to 18, more than twice the legal limit. As one staffer put it, "It's pretty much the Assembly policy not to increase penalties." Paterson was said to be looking to broker a deal to make the blood alcohol limit for a felony 13. Rosado and senators, including Fuschillo and Democrat Martin Dilan, pressed the Assembly not to make any alterations.

As Albany slewed, waiting for a budget deal, Rosado got more attention for his cause. Finally Assembly Speaker Sheldon Silver agreed to the legislation. "I give the father full credit for shaming Shelly," said Sen. Frank Padayan. Assemblyman Harvey Weisenberg, the bill's sponsor in the Assembly, said it wasn't shame that brought Silver around but lively debate. "They say it's three men in the room, but in the Assembly there are 108 people, and we all get our opportunity to speak. It's sort of like group therapy. I told them there is no reason to change the law from what is real!" Weisenberg said.

Some Assembly members worry the penalty might be too harsh and that the bill did not receive enough scrutiny. Assembly member Vito Lopez told the *New York Times*, "I believe there are a lot of voices who would like to be heard. They will never be heard, and the reason they will never be heard is because there's too much emotionalism."

Raising Awareness

On the Senate floor, a number of senators who supported the legislation acknowledged that the bill will not necessarily stop drunk people from driving with children in the car. Revealing that her parents were alcoholics, Sen. Diane Savino said that the bill will not fix everything because alcoholics "are incapable of rational thought." She said she hoped the bill would raise awareness and make people more cautious of who children get into the car with.

Critics also have raised concerns about the efficacy of the interlocks. They say the devices aren't sensitive enough to always properly recognize the amount of alcohol in a person's system and can sometimes mistake other substances for alcohol. Drivers can use an alternative vehicle to avoid the interlock, and there also privacy issues.

A study by the Insurance Institute for Highway Safety found interlocks can help prevent repeat offenses, but most fatal alcohol-related crashes do not involve someone who had been convicted of drunk driving within the past three years. That has spurred some advocates to cell for the use of interlocks in all vehicles.

Making it a felony will go a long way to deterring people from driving while they are drunk.

Whatever the bill's shortcomings might be, Kate Hogan, director of the District Attorney's Association of the State of New York, said she didn't "dare to dream" that a bill that would both up the penalty for drinking and driving with a child in the car and require the use of interlocks in the vehicles of those convicted of driving while intoxicated could actually be passed during the current special session.

Advocates say there is much more to do.

"Making it a felony will go a long way to deterring people from driving while they are drunk," said Sen. Hiram Monserrate, a former police officer. But he noted that New York City has had problems prosecuting suspected cases of drunk driving and pointed to recent cases in which police officers refused breathalyzer tests after killing people with their cars. "It's harder to get the evidence you need for a prosecution than you might think," said Monserrate.

Breath and Blood

In September [2009] at 1 o'clock on a Sunday morning, officer Andrew Kelly of the 68th precinct struck and killed Vionique Valnord as she tried to hail a cab in Brooklyn. A sergeant at the scene reportedly saw alcoholic beverages in Kelly's vehicle, smelled alcohol and reported that Kelly's speech was slurred. Kelly initially refused a breath test. It took seven hours for police to secure a warrant to force Kelly to submit to a test, and when he did he tested clean.

Only a month later, Detective Kevin Spellman struck and killed 67-year-old Drana Nikac in the Bronx. Responding officers reported that Spellman appeared intoxicated, but Spellman refused a breath test at the scene. He eventually submitted to one at a hospital, five hours later. Even, then, officials have said Spellman had a blood alcohol level of .21, more than two and a half times the legal limits.

Police Commissioner Ray Kelly has created a panel to consider how to handle instances when someone refused a test. Currently police generally take a person who won't take a test at the scene to the precinct. If the driver refuses the test there, police must obtain a warrant to allow blood to be drawn at a hospital. That can take hours.

Some advocates would like the legislature to remove the warrant requirement for Breathalyzer use in cases where someone has died or been seriously injured.

Not all children who die on the streets are killed by drunk drivers.

Hogan, Fuschillo and Weisenberg say they see one particular piece of legislation as being paramount: Jack Shea's law, which would remove the state requirement that a doctor supervise a blood draw. Shea, a 91-year-old former Olympian, was killed in upstate New York by a driver who was charged with driving while intoxicated, vehicular manslaughter and criminally negligent homicide. The charges were eventually dropped over a technicality. The driver wound up in a rural clinic where a technician drew a blood sample to check alcohol levels without the supervision of a doctor.

Fuschillo said he had assurances from Paterson that he wants to move on that bill. Paterson's office did not return calls for comment.

Rosado isn't giving up the fight, either. He announced at the signing of the bill named for his daughter that he intends to try to take his campaign to make driving under the influence with a minor in the vehicle national. "This is not going to be our last stop," Rosado promised. Later, he added, "I guarantee you that my daughter's death will not be in vain. She is here now to protect all our children, and anyone else who is a victim of DWI."

When Bad Driving Turns Deadly

Not all children who die on the streets are killed by drunk drivers. The parents of Hayley Ng, age 4, and Diego Martinez, 3, know that all too well. Their children died on a Chinatown sidewalk in January when an unoccupied delivery van plowed into a group of children on a school outing. The driver, Chao Fu, left the van idling without realizing it was in reverse. He did not face any criminal charges.

Some 292 people—including people in cars, on bicycles and on foot—died in traffic fatalities in 2008, an increase from 2007, which saw a record low 274 such deaths.

Bad or reckless driving causes many of these deaths and many more injuries. Speeding and inattentiveness are the leading causes, according to Wiley Norvell of Transportation Alternatives, an advocacy group.

"Notwithstanding the outrageous and tragic death of Leandra, and the egregious and tragic 'Taconic Mom' incident, the number of people killed and maimed as a result of adults driving drunk with minors is dwarfed by the numbers killed and maimed by more mundane but often lethal behaviors such as turning into pedestrians in crosswalks (the documented number one 'mode' of pedestrian fatality in NYC), aggressive passing of bicyclists (the documented number one 'mode' of cyclist fatality in NYC). and of course the run-of-the-mill speeding, red-light running, distracted driving, aggressive driving, etc.," Charles Komanoff, a long-time transportation activist, wrote in an email.

The number of these cases that result in criminal, let alone felony, charges remain minuscule. Examples abound. Chehebar reached a plea agreement and served only four months in jail.

Alexander Aponte was driving a campaign bus for a candidate for City Council—even though his license had been suspended. He ran a red light and killed 9-year-old Ibrahim Ahmed. Aponte got off with a misdemeanor charge: driving with a suspended license.

Attorney Robert Fader said he handled one case where a driver and a bicyclist had a dispute on the road, prompting the driver to deliberately back up and run down the cyclist. The driver's only penalty was a ticket for leaving the scene of a crime.

"If somebody is drunk, they'll be prosecuted, but if someone is driving without a license they'll get a ticket," Fader said, "You can't arrest people who are negligent."

Legal Barriers

In New York, people whose bad, but sober, driving kills someone can face a charge of criminally negligent homicide. But courts, law enforcement and relatives of victims rarely concur on when a traffic death becomes a criminal act.

Reckless behavior is not generally viewed as criminally negligent, according to attorney Barton Slavin. "I don't know where the line is drawn," he said. Earlier this fall, a jury in Manhattan convicted Auvryn Scarlett, a garbage truck driver, of second-degree murder. Scarlett struck and killed two British tourists last winter after he apparently neglected to take his epilepsy medicine. At the time, Komanoff said he could not recall any other instance when a driver who was not intoxicated was convicted of murder.

Why here? A police spokesman said, "Apparently, he stopped taking his medication, it was a conscious decision, so he's being charged."

But Paul Steely White, executive director of Transportation Alternatives, failed to see the distinction. "Don't people make a conscious decision to speed or a conscious decision to turn without yielding?" he said in Streetsblog. "Are we saying that people are somehow unconscious when they're breaking the law? . . . Scarlett's actions were no more deliberate than the majority of negligent motorists who routinely get off scot-free."

A variety of factors—public attitudes, prosecutorial and police practices and judicial rulings—have have combined to create leniency. Deaths caused by reckless drivers—not drunk ones—"have not receive the grassroots consciousness raising" that alcohol related accidents have gotten, said Maureen McCormick, chief of Vehicular Crimes in Nassau County. While the public has become increasingly aware of the risks posed by dangerous drivers, the criminal justice system lags behind, she said: "It's like turning around a battleship."

Prosecutors, according to Slavin, may be reluctant to bring cases in traffic deaths because the likelihood of getting a felony conviction is slim. Unless an officer saw the accident proving it involved, for example, going 60 in a 30 mile per hour zone may be difficult.

The 'Rule of Two' Favors Reckless Drivers

Then there is the so-called "rule of two." Although not actually a law, this rule—more a kind of practice or belief, really—holds that drivers who are not drunk cannot be prosecuted for criminally negligent homicide unless they did two things wrong: speeding and running a red light, for example, rather than committing just one of those offenses.

Two recent Court Ruling in New York have raised the bar even higher, according to McCormick. In one, the Court of Appeals, the state's highest court, overturned the conviction of Brett Cabrera, a 17-year-old with a junior license who had killed three passengers in his car. The court found he had been speeding and violating the terms of his junior license. Despite that, it threw out his conviction.

"Our decisions have uniformly locked for some kind of morally blameworthy component to excessive speed in determining criminal negligence," the court said. That, it continued, did not appear in Cabrera's case.

Proponents of tougher penalties hoped the court had given Cabrera a break because of his age, McCormick said. Then came a second ruling involving limousine driver James McGrantham. After realizing he had entered the Belt Parkway via an exit ramp and so was head the wrong way, McGrantham decided to make a three-point turn in the middle of the highway. As he performed this maneuver, his car stretched across traffic creating a kind of wall. A motorcyclist, unable to stop, crashed into that barrier and died.

The Court of Appeals threw out that homicide conviction, McCormick said, because the limo driver had not acted with malevolence. Or as a the court phrased it, "Driver was sober, not speeding, and the decision to extricate himself from a dangerous situation while unwise was not morally blameworthy so as to support criminally negligent homicide."

McCormick believes such interpretations have gone beyond what the legislature intended. To correct that, she said, the legislature may have to step in and clarify its laws.

Some advocates have endorsed another piece of legislation, this one proposed by Assemblymember Robert Sweeney, that would make vehicular assault and manslaughter felonies if the driver involved had a suspended or revoked license. Sweeney proposed his bill after the death of Ibrahim Ahmed.

Whether prosecutors would use harsher laws remains unclear. And would juries be willing to convict a generally law-abiding person for the mistake of running a red light—even if that mistake had horrible consequences. As McCormick puts it these kinds of crimes "are committed by average Joes."

Preventive Measures

Undoubtedly, though, average Joes commit such offenses very frequently. Anyone who drives—or walks—in New York City knows how often drivers shoot red lights or fail to yield to pedestrians. Some 30 percent of drivers exceed the 30 mile per hour speed limit in Manhattan, according to a Transportation Alternatives study released earlier this year. While most were going 40 miles per hour or less, the study found people driving "in excess of 60 mph in school zones and other areas with heavy pedestrian traffic."

"It's New York and everyone wants to get there in a hurry," said Slavin. "If people would just slow down and act less crazed and come to a stop at a stop sign," fewer people would be injured in accidents.

Transportation Alternatives has locked at some of New York's most dangerous intersections and urged the police to focus on them. Norvell likens this to the way the city has reduced crime.

There is no second chance on the road.

Manhattan Borough President Scott Stringer has called for installing speeding and red light enforcement cameras.

The incoming Manhattan district attorney, Cyrus Vance, has said he would establish a Vehicular Crime Unit that would, among other things, pay special attention to dangerous intersections or stretches of road. It also would focus on traffic assaults, reckless driving and other roadway offenses. He has also said his office would work with the police to reduce speeding in Manhattan.

"There is no second chance on the road—when a car crashes and someone is killed—no apology, no claim that it was strictly an accident, will ever bring that loved one back," Vance said in response to a questionnaire during the campaign. As a result, he continued, "strong preventative measures must be taken by police and prosecutors with the ultimate goal of reducing incidents of dangerous driving."

All of this assumes that people are ready to take bad driving seriously. Norvell and McCormick think that can happen.

"A generation ago, somebody who was caught drinking and driving was sent home with a wink," Norvell said. Leandra's law provides evidence of just how much that has changed. Now, said Norvell, "the way we tolerate and encourage dangerous and reckless driving on our streets is in need of a similar cultural shift."

2

DUI Laws Are Discriminatory and Do Not Prevent Drunk Driving

Nick Pinto

Nick Pinto is a staff writer for the Minneapolis City Pages.

Too many drunk driving convictions in Minnesota have led to a decrease in social stigma for offenders. Moreover, while creating revenue for the state and for defense lawyers, drunk driving laws have failed to make roads safer. For every 100 offenses, only one person is caught. Worse, the laws have become so complex and complicated, that citizens can't navigate legal proceedings against them. Yet defense lawyers are often prohibitively expensive. While everybody wants to keep motorists safe, the real problem might be alcoholism, an ill that no police force can solve.

A ngela was arrested for waiting in her car.

It was a hot night last summer, and she had gone out drinking in New Hope with two of her friends. She'd driven to the bar, but by the end of the night, she knew she'd had too much to drink. After racking up three DWI [driving while intoxicated] offenses in her early 20s, Angela was on the straight and narrow. She didn't want to get another. She wanted to be responsible.

Angela isn't her real name, but she doesn't want to reveal her identity because admitting to drunk driving is embarrass-

Nick Pinto, "One in Seven Minnesotans Has a Drunk Driving Conviction. Are We Any Safer?" CityPages.com, June 9, 2010. Reproduced by permission of the author.

ing. "There's a stigma to it," she says. "I don't want people at work to know that about me."

So instead of driving home, Angela and her friends called a taxi. While they were waiting, they sat in her parked car, smoking cigarettes and talking about music.

Over the Legal Limit

Big mistake. Within a few minutes, a policeman was rapping at her window, asking her to step out of the car and take a field sobriety test. She failed. She took the breath test, and failed that too, blowing a .10.

"I kept explaining, 'I'm not driving, we're not going anywhere, we're waiting for a taxi, he'll be here any minute,'" Angela says.

But it didn't matter. She was over the legal limit while behind the wheel. Under the "physical control" provision of Minnesota's DWI law, she was guilty. As the cab pulled up to take her friends home, she was hauled away to be booked for her fourth DWI, a felony offense that can carry up to seven years in prison.

First-time offenders lose their licenses for 90 days.

Welcome to the world of drunk driving enforcement in Minnesota. In the state law books, the first-degree murder statute takes up three quarters of a page; the section on drunk driving takes up 40 pages. With more than 100 people killed and thousands injured by drunk driving every year in the state, no one feels sorry for the reckless people who get behind the wheel when they shouldn't.

But there are reasons to question whether the current strategy of busting as many people as possible and piling on the punishment is working. The legal system is choked with impaired driving cases. Advocates for the poor say the system hits them especially hard. More and more Minnesotans are carrying a scarlet DWI in their files, paying several times the normal insurance premiums, and struggling to figure out how they're going to get to work without a license.

The costs of the war on drunk driving are real. So is it working?

DWI activists say it is, and point to a 38 percent drop in the number of alcohol-related fatalities on Minnesota roads in the last 25 years. But that statistic doesn't tell the whole story. Non-alcohol-related fatalities have also been steadily dropping for years, the result of improved road conditions, safer cars, and the adoption of seatbelts and airbags. Twenty-five years ago, more than 600 people died in crashes in Minnesota. In 2008, the last year for which figures are available, that number was down to 455—a 25 percent drop. The fact is, when you look at the proportion of traffic deaths and injuries in the state that can be blamed on alcohol, the numbers have hardly budged in the last 10 years, stubbornly sticking between 30 and 40 percent. By this measurement, drunk driving is as much of a problem as ever.

For those who do get caught, the consequences are severe. First-time offenders lose their licenses for 90 days. In the metro area, taxis and public transportation make this an inconvenience at worst. But in most of the state, getting to work, to the grocery store, or to pick up the kids at preschool is impossible if you don't have a car. After the suspension is over, drivers have to pay a $700 reinstatement fee. Then they can also expect their insurance premiums to go up by a factor of three or four.

The Stigma of a DWI Is Being Removed

For more than a decade, Minnesota cops have been handing out DWIs at the rate of more than 30,000 a year. Over time, all those write-ups pile up. Nearly one in seven drivers in Minnesota has a DWI on his or her record. In our effort to make drunk driving unacceptable, we may be in danger of doing the opposite. If nearly everyone knows someone with a DWI, how much stigma does it carry?

Not so long ago, Minnesota was a drunk driver's paradise. As late as 1959, it was perfectly legal to keep an open handle of vodka between your legs as you drove down the highway. Even if you were pulled over on suspicion of being drunk, you could refuse to take a blood-alcohol test, effectively denying the cops the evidence they would need to charge you.

The result, as you might expect, was a bloodbath of alcohol-related crashes.

"We were literally killing 300 people a year in Minnesota. And for every person killed, there were about 20 injured," says Steve Simon, a professor at the University of Minnesota Law School and an anti-drunk-driving crusader. "It was a serious, serious public health problem."

In the 1960s, the state decided it needed to get tough on drunk driving. It passed the Implied Consent Law, which said that when you get your license and drive on Minnesota roads, you've implicitly agreed to be tested if the police think it's warranted. If you refused a test, you lost your license for six months. The Legislature also made it much easier to prove drunkenness, with a law decreeing that if your blood alcohol concentration was over .10 percent you were intoxicated, even if you weren't obviously impaired.

The laws continued to tighten in the 1970s. Driving with a concentration of .10 percent went from being evidence of intoxication to being outright illegal, a misdemeanor on its own.

Minnesota also pioneered a new strategy, becoming the first state to set up a parallel civil penalty alongside the criminal penalties: If you tested over the limit, the commissioner of public safety would revoke your license for 90 days. Eventually, this new administrative process was streamlined to the point that police could revoke your license on the spot, without having to first file paperwork with the commissioner, and before you ever saw the inside of a courtroom. At first you could delay the instant revocation by asking for a hearing to challenge it, but in 1982 that loophole was closed as well. You could still fight to get your license back in a judicial hearing, but while you were waiting you wouldn't be able to drive.

In 2004, the legal alcohol limit was dropped to .08 percent. And the movement to get stricter is far from over: Nearly every year, the Legislature considers a raft of new provisions to tighten the screws.

A Moral Trump Card

The driving force behind this escalating war on drunk drivers has been the state chapter of Mothers Against Drunk Driving, the national organization founded in 1980. Any group fighting for stiffer DWI penalties has an advantage out of the gate— who's going to stand up for going easy on drunk drivers?— but the Mothers carry a moral trump card. Their founder and much of their membership are mothers whose children have been killed by drunk drivers.

Leveraging this high ground, MADD successfully pushed to lower the blood alcohol limit to .08 percent in every state in the union. They fight for random roadblock checkpoints, higher beer taxes, and keeping the legal drinking age at 21.

With law enforcement budgets threadbare, there are hardly enough cops on the road to offer a credible challenge to all the state's drunk drivers.

In Minnesota, much of MADD's lobbying muscle has been flexed through the DWI Task Force, a group of law enforcement officials and activists that proposes new laws to combat drunk driving.

A 2006 report by the task force sums up the group's philosophy: "The most effective general deterrent action a state can take is to maintain a high level of DWI arrests."

Of course, with law enforcement budgets threadbare, there are hardly enough cops on the road to offer a credible challenge to all the state's drunk drivers. Chances are, if you try to make it home from the bar, you're not going to be stopped.

"Statistically, you have to drive about 100 times in this state to be arrested once for DWI," says Steve Simon, the law professor who founded the DWI Task Force. "That's why the penalty needs to be substantial. The consequences need to be so great that people think twice about driving even if they're unlikely to be caught."

But Jeffrey Sheridan, a DWI defense lawyer who attends the Task Force meetings, says the group's quest for arrests and stiff penalties has gotten out of control. Tall, with well-coiffed white hair and blue eyes, Sheridan moves and talks with the self-assurance of a trial lawyer. As one of the state's top DWI defense attorneys, he has made a career charging clients top dollar to beat their drunk-driving raps.

Pushing Back Against Activists

"For many years, I was very cynical about it," Sheridan says. "I watched the penalties pile up and the laws become more byzantine, and every time the Legislature changed the law it was more work for me. This business has been very good to me."

But more recently, Sheridan has started to push back against MADD.

"I call them the Mad Mothers," Sheridan says. "They've got enormous political capital with no real counterweight. They just keep pushing laws through, ratcheting up the penalties, to the point where they've done an end-run around our Constitutional rights."

If you want to understand why nearly one in seven Minnesotan drivers has a DWI, a good place to start is the Implied Consent law. Every year, Minnesota police revoke between 30,000 and 40,000 licenses by the side of the road, before the drivers can even talk to a lawyer, let alone plead their case to a judge or a jury of their peers. Even if the suspect can prove he wasn't intoxicated, he may still wind up with a DWI on his record.

You can challenge your license revocation, but unless you read the fine print legalese on the back of the form the police make you sign, you won't know that you only have 30 days to do it. And since the court dates for the criminal charges often aren't set until after that period, by the time many people are talking to a lawyer, it's already too late. Once the deadline has passed, you've got a DWI on your record, even if you beat the criminal charges.

It's hard to find a lawyer in Minnesota who'll represent a DWI case for less than $500.

"It's a crazy system," Sheridan says. "A DWI is a criminal offense, and in this country, when you're [charged with] a crime, you're supposed to get your day in court."

But what some people find even more troubling is that the two-track system of parallel criminal and civil penalties appears to be stacked against the poor and indigent. It's hard to find a lawyer in Minnesota who'll represent a DWI case for less than $500. Those who can't afford a lawyer for their criminal case get assigned a public defender. But public defenders, by law, can only represent their clients in criminal cases. Since the implied consent hearing is civil, if you can't afford a lawyer, you'll be going head-to-head with the state with no one to represent you. And implied consent hearings aren't the kind of thing you want to muddle through on your own.

An Unfair Legal System

"If you don't have a lawyer, you're going to lose," Sheridan says. "There are a few cases where someone wins representing themselves, but it almost never happens."

Between the quick deadline and the long odds for people without counsel, it's not surprising that about nine out of every ten drivers never even challenge their license revocation in an implied consent hearing.

"The system is entirely unfair to the people who can't afford counsel," says Travis Schwantes, the chief public defender for the 10th Judicial District. "We're always trying to persuade our clients that the system is fair, that win or lose, justice is being done. But when I explain to clients that it's too late, or that we can't represent them on the civil side, they walk away feeling tricked and cheated."

Defense attorneys and civil liberties activists aren't the only ones who question the wisdom of Minnesota's civil DWI penalties. The program has also drawn criticism from within the criminal justice system. With crippling state budget cuts and the judiciary fighting to keep every penny of funding it can, some say running suspected drunk drivers through criminal and civil courts to get a DWI on their records doesn't make financial sense.

"It's a big waste of money. We're basically paying for two separate legal systems where one will do," says a lawyer who didn't want to be named because of his ongoing work as a city attorney. "You have city and county attorneys trying the criminal cases, and then there's this completely duplicative civil process run out of the Attorney General's Office."

In the last legislative session, Rep. Tom Emmer (R-Delano) introduced a bill to eliminate all the pretrial civil penalties for accused drunk drivers. But the Legislature had no appetite to take on MADD. The bill bounced between committees and never made it to the floor. (Emmer, whose own DWIs became an issue in the run-up to his endorsement as the GOP candidate for governor, declined to talk about the issue.)

Technology Is Used Against Repeat Offenders

On May 18, [2010] Governor Pawlenty signed a bill to install ignition interlock systems in the cars of some DWI offenders, radically reshaping the debate. The technology requires drivers to pass one breath test before they can start their car, and another five minutes later to make sure drivers aren't enlisting sober friends to get the car rolling.

Under the new law, which goes into effect next July, ignition interlocks will be mandatory in the cars of repeat drunk drivers and first-time offenders caught with a blood alcohol level over .16 percent.

The adoption of the ignition interlock devices was remarkable because it scrambled the familiar battle lines. Everyone liked it. MADD supported it because it keeps drunk drivers off the road. Critics of the punishment-heavy model liked it because it lets people who have made a mistake keep driving legally.

"It was a paradigm shift," says Jean Ryan, the alcohol programs coordinator at the Department of Public Safety. "Technology gave us a tool we didn't have before, and it's changing how we approach the problem."

Of course, the ignition interlock program has some familiar vulnerabilities. Just as someone with a suspended license can decide to drive anyway, DWI offenders under the new regime can still break the law and hop in a car that doesn't have a device installed.

But experts are optimistic that scientific innovations are going to keep changing how the state fights drunk driving.

Ever since the law started emphasizing blood alcohol content as the critical factor in judging intoxication, law enforcement has looked for reliable ways to test it.

"I think it's just a matter of time before we see this and other technologies coming standard on every vehicle," Sheridan says. "We're going to see the same adoption process that happened with seat belts and air bags."

But those developments are still a long way off, and there are other reasons to be wary of leaning on fancy gear as a panacea. You don't have to look any further than the state's ongoing battle over the Intoxilyzer 5000 to see the potential pitfalls.

Ever since the law started emphasizing blood alcohol content as the critical factor in judging intoxication, law enforcement has looked for reliable ways to test it. The most accurate method, of course, is to test the blood itself, but getting a rowdy drunk to submit to a finger prick is asking for trouble, so over the years police have relied on breath and urine tests. Most states have stopped allowing urine tests, since drivers can piss positive long after they're sober. Since 1997, Minnesota police have been using a breath-test machine manufactured by Kentucky-based CMI Inc.

Breathalyzers Might Be Faulty

The problem with CMI's Intoxilyzer 5000 is that it's black box: You blow into it and a reading comes out, but what happens in between is a secret. The technology has never had a full validation study, and CMI won't disclose how the Intoxilyzer works.

In 2006 and 2007, two Minnesotans charged with drunk driving challenged the Intoxilyzer. If they were going to suffer the penalty for drunk driving, they argued in court, they should at least be able to examine the software that was sealing their fate. The courts agreed, and the state ordered CMI to turn over its source code for evaluation. CMI balked, resulting in a stalemate that persists to this day. In the meantime, hundreds of Minnesotans have used the same argument, creating a massive backlog of unresolved DWI cases that continues to grow.

"The Intoxilyzer case shows the problems with relying too much on technology," Sheridan says. "It's not a silver bullet."

Pretty much everyone in the DWI debate agrees that the problem with attacking drunk driving is that drunk driving isn't the real problem. The real problem is drinking.

"To really address drunk driving, you have to address drinking," says Simon. "And that's something that's deeply ingrained in our culture. Western society has been using alcohol for 7,000 years. It's something we're very resistant to changing."

An Alcohol Tax Increase Might Help

Simon thinks the best way to put a dent in drunk driving and all the other alcohol-related ills is to jack up the taxes on alcohol and make the industry and consumers pay for all the social services their drinks necessitate. But resistance to that plan—from the alcohol industry, from liquor stores, from bars, and from Minnesotans who like to drink—will be substantial. Change will be incremental.

"It's something we can effect, bit by bit, through education," says Jean Mulvey, the executive director of MADD in Minnesota. "Look at what happened with cigarettes. These things can change."

In the meantime, though, people like Angela will keep getting arrested. Thousands of Minnesotans a year will get DWIs on their records without ever being convicted of a crime. And the poor will face the legal maze alone.

"Drunk driving is horrible, everyone wants to get rid of it," says Travis Schwantes, the public defender. "But in doing that, we have to make sure that our process is fair. Everybody in MADD, every law enforcement officer, has a friend or relative that's been picked up on a DWI. We want our friends and family to be treated fairly. It isn't just the people who are habitually driving drunk, it's our friends and relatives. It's us."

Drunk Driving by Women Is on the Rise

Portland Press Herald

The Portland Press Herald *is a daily newspaper out of Portland, Maine.*

While male alcohol consumption is widely accepted, women often drink in secrecy to avoid being stigmatized. If they develop problems, they are less likely to be detected. That is why the increasing number of female drunk drivers has caught many by surprise. Yet women are responsible for an ever higher number of traffic fatalities, and while men are still the main culprits, female drunk drivers present a problem that should be taken seriously.

Two stories this month [March 2010] should shake up the way that we think about drunk driving and how to prevent it.

Last week the U.S. Transportation Department released statistics that show a nearly 30 percent rise over the last two decades in the number of arrests of women for driving under the influence of drugs or alcohol. During the same period, the number of arrests of men for the same offenses dropped 7.5 percent.

The second story was the tragic death of eight people in Westchester County, New York, where Dianne Schuler, a mother with alcohol and marijuana in her system, drove the

"Drunk Driving by Women Requires New Tactics," *Portland Press Herald*, March 10, 2010. Reprinted with permission of Portland Press Herald/Maine Sunday Telegram. Reproduction does not imply endorsement.

wrong way for two miles before colliding with another vehicle, killing herself, her 2-year-old daughter, three young nieces and three men. Friends and family members were shocked to hear that her blood contained twice the legal limit of alcohol.

There is a more damning social stigma for women who abuse alcohol, so they are more likely to pick times when no one else is around to drink, and take steps to control their appearance.

The two stories hammer home the point that men and women are both in danger of abusing drugs and alcohol, but for a variety of reasons can respond to it in different ways. And while public information and law enforcement efforts have had some success in discouraging men from getting behind the wheel when they should not, they are not working as well with women.

Drinking In Secrecy

In the wake of the Taconic Parkway crash, substance abuse experts interviewed in *The New York Times* said that not all alcoholics are the same.

Women, it was reported, are much more likely to be secret drinkers, adept at hiding their abuse from family, friends and coworkers. There is a more damning social stigma for women who abuse alcohol, so they are more likely to pick times when no one else is around to drink, and take steps to control their appearance.

Others become adept at hiding liquor and sneaking it into social settings in innocuous packaging. Addicts are notoriously successful at deceiving the people around them into believing that they don't have a problem.

If no one knows that a woman is drinking, efforts to enlist others to stop them from driving, like the "Friends don't let friends drive drunk" campaign, won't work.

In an op-ed column in this newspaper Aug. 15, Polly Haight Frawley of Crossroads for Women, a substance abuse treatment program in Portland, said that the subterfuge is effective.

She cited studies that show that children of addicted fathers learn about his problem at about age 12. They don't learn about a mother's addiction until they are 18. And despite changes in the way families divide responsibilities over the last several decades, women are still much more likely to care for children, meaning that they are also more likely to be driving them around. That puts those children in danger.

More Studies Are Needed

There is a good reason that men are the focus of most law enforcement efforts to curb drunk driving. Males are still more than three times as likely to be caught drunk behind the wheel and still pose a significant public safety threat.

But the strategies that work for men may not work for women, who could be drinking in secret during the day instead of in a bar and so might be less likely to be caught by a late-night road block.

Clearly this is a problem that needs more study and a deeper understanding so that more lives, like the eight who died in New York, are not needlessly wasted.

4

Female Alcoholism Is a Growing Safety Concern

Amelia Kunhardt

Amelia Kunhardt is an award-winning multimedia journalist at the Patriot Ledger, *out of Quincy, Massachusetts.*

The real problem behind the rise of female drunk drivers is alcoholism. While male alcohol abuse has been acknowledged for many decades, female alcoholics have lived outside the public eye. Yet since mothers are often the primary caretakers of children and mostly responsible for driving their kids to school and sports practices, more and more often they get caught with illegal blood alcohol levels. The problem of alcoholism must be treated in order to reduce drunk driving fatalities.

Maggie Towne wore one shoe and held an empty purse as Braintree police led her into the station.

After a night out drinking with a friend, she was busted and, she realized with sudden clarity, broken.

"That's how my whole life was at that point, just scattered and picking it back up piece by piece," Towne, 27, and single, recalls of the early hours of Oct. 10, 2009, after she crossed the center line on Forbes Road and hit an oncoming car head-on.

Melissa Perry can't even draw on her recollection of her drunken-driving arrest on June 21, 2009. After spending $5 for a half-pint of Yukon Jack and downing 8 ounces of 100--

proof whiskey in a half-hour, she recalls falling asleep in bed. Her next memory—in a blackout, she got up, left her house and crashed her car on Swift's Beach Road in Wareham—was waking up in a CAT scan machine at Wareham's Tobey Hospital.

"It cost me a loss of self-worth. We're drinking away our problems, like I did that day," said Perry, 39, a divorced mother of four. "That five dollars was going to solve my problems that night. It didn't."

Alcohol Abuse Among Women Is on The Rise

Each story is unique for the growing number of women—like Towne and Perry, nationally and in Massachusetts—who get caught drinking and driving. But one common thread among them is that such arrests often reflect a larger, and likewise growing problem—of women abusing alcohol.

"I assume when a person gets arrested for drinking and driving, it's not the first time," said Sarah Allen Benton, a mental health counselor who practices in Norwell and Belmont. "Not everyone is an alcoholic who gets pulled over, but there is (often) some issue around alcohol that needs to be addressed."

Stereotypically, it's men who go to bars, drink heavily, then get caught. But more and more women, from all walks of life, are themselves struggling with alcohol-related issues.

"The public may have a perception . . . of what a woman impaired or a drunken driver looks like," said Hingham police Sgt. Steven Dearth. "We find all (women)—upper class, lower class, poor, rich, all ages."

In the United States, 17.6 million people—about 1 in every 12 adults—abuse alcohol or are alcohol dependent, according to the National Institute on Alcohol Abuse and Alcoholism. And the percentage of those who are women is rising:

about 5.9 million, or 5.1 percent of adult female Americans, needed treatment in 2008 for alcohol problems.

Problems Can Develop Early

Conrad Schulz sees many such women, as director of the driver alcohol education program at High Point Treatment Center, which has offices in Plymouth, Brockton, New Bedford and Taunton. About 80 to 85 percent of those who attend his classes at the center have "some degree of a problem with alcohol, ranging from just beginning to have problems to third-stage, chronic alcoholic," he said.

Problems with alcohol often start early. Even if the first sips didn't go down easily the first time Towne drank beer—at age 15—she went on to down seven bottles. By 12 years later, things had changed. When she drank, she'd often get violent and lash out, then wake up the next day feeling "overwhelming guilt."

"A lot more shame came into my life, as my drinking progressed," Towne said.

A mother at 16 and new wife at 17, Perry started drinking in her late teens. She said she stopped not long afterward, when her alcohol use "got out of control." But she resumed drinking a few years later, and by her mid-30s, her alcohol use had "just built into a monster," she said, that affected most of her waking life.

That includes drinking and driving the night of her arrest, of which she remembers little.

"It's a blackout moment," she said, grateful no one was hurt in the crash two blocks from her house. "Everyone else has seen it, read about it, and I have no clue. It's embarrassing."

More women, like men, are getting caught drinking and driving again and again. As for Towne and Perry, they said that judges' orders, as well as embarrassment, have had their effect and both said they haven't drunk since their arrest. But that hardly means their struggle with alcohol—and conversely, how it affects others, including on the road—is anywhere near over.

I can't live with somebody else dying because of my alcoholism.

"Do I think about it? I do," said Perry. "The cost is too high for a five-dollar drink. You can't undo what I did."

Regret and Shame Linger

Towne has found support—and company—in a mutual help group that, she said, includes "people who genuinely give a damn because they're exactly where I've been, I am, I was. And they're there with me."

No one was seriously hurt in her crash, either. But the fact someone could have been led Towne to think, "If you don't stop now, you're going to kill somebody. . . . I can't live with somebody else dying because of my alcoholism."

For now, many women are living with alcoholism. Towne, for one, said that she's making progress in identifying the underlying causes of her drinking as well as the consequences—including the innocent woman whom she hit last year.

"I want to see this girl who I hit," said Towne. "She is not somebody who I just put in the back of my mind, and never thought of again. And say, I'm sorry."

5

The Problem of Drunk Driving by Women Is Being Distorted

Kate Harding

Kate Harding is the founder of the blog Shapely Prose. She has been a regular contributor to Salon.com's Broadsheet column.

Recent reports about the increasing number of traffic accidents caused by drunk female drivers are vastly overstated. While drunk driving accidents among women are up, women still account for a fraction of fatalities. The misleading interpretations of statistics are politically motivated, trying to reinforce "proper" behavior for women, warning females to not aspire to threaten the male domain of power.

L et me begin by saying that the last thing on earth I want to do is minimize the seriousness of drunk driving or the devastation it can wreak. When I was seven, my family was hit head-on by a drunk driver who turned a corner into the wrong lane because he was busy trying to throw his passenger out of the car. One of my dearest friends lost her brother to a drunk driving accident—and years later, the driver killed himself the same way. So believe me when I tell you, I am no apologist for people who get behind the wheel when there's *any* chance they're too impaired to handle it.

I am, however, a feminist, which makes me immediately skeptical of articles like one today from the Associated Press,

Kate Harding, "When Women Act Like Men, Children Die," Salon.com, August 7, 2009. This article first appeared in Salon.com, at http://www.salon.com. An online version remains in the Salon archives. Reprinted with permission.

identifying "disturbing trends" that happen to further extremely trendy Bad Mommy narratives and include such trenchant sociological analysis as "Women are picking up some of the dangerously bad habits of men" (from Mothers Against Drunk Driving CEO Chuck Hurley). Beginning with the tragic example of Diane Schuler, who recently drove the wrong way down a one-way street with a blood alcohol level of 0.19, causing an accident that killed eight people (including herself and four children), the article goes on to inform us that more women are reporting that they drink heavily, more women are being arrested for drunk driving and, like Schuler, some of them even drive drunk with their kids in the car—which Hurley calls "the ultimate form of child abuse."

Misleading Use of Statistics

The numbers, however, tell a much less alarming story. Though this does represent an increase over previous years, in California, only 18.8 percent of DUI arrests are women. By my calculations, that means 81.2 percent are *not* women. And we have to extrapolate from California data because the nationwide number of female drunk driving arrests isn't included; we're only told that it was "28.8 percent higher in 2007 than it was in 1998, while the number of men arrested was 7.5 percent lower"—which sounds shocking until you consider that we're also supposed to be shocked by how the number of women aged 30 to 44 who self-report alcohol abuse has *more than doubled*: jumping all the way up to 3.3 percent. Also, we should probably factor in "[a]nother possible reason cited for the rising arrests: Police are less likely to let women off the hook these days." There's that. As for women drivers putting their kids at risk, "Arrests of drunken mothers with children in the car remain rare, but police officers can generally list a few." Oh well, then.

So what we have here is a trend of *statistically* significant increases in the number of women arrested for drunk driving

and the number of women who say they abuse alcohol—
neither of which is a solid indicator of the number of drunk
women on the road, given police discretion in making arrests
and the notorious unreliability of self-reported data—which is
being spun into a socially significant trend: Women are turning into a bunch of alcoholic narcissists who must be stopped!
Think of the children!

---

*Fewer than 3 percent of women overall report abusing
alcohol.*

That image is reinforced by anecdotes about women who
have driven with extremely high blood alcohol levels and children on board—including one who'd been clubbing with her
teenage daughter, the harlot—and a lot of hand-wringing
about how *male* that sort of behavior is. In addition to
Hurley's "dangerously bad habits" quote, we have Chris Co-
chran of the California Office of Traffic Safety saying: "Younger
women feel more empowered, more equal to men, and have
been beginning to exhibit the same uninhibited behaviors as
men." Reader, you heard it here first: Equality kills. I love how
those quotes simultaneously demonize women and highlight
the far more prevalent problem: men driving drunk. "Men
still drink more than women and are responsible for more
drunken-driving cases," says the article. "But the gap is nar-
rowing." OK, well, maybe let me know when the gap gets a
little narrower than 80/20.

False Alarm

Let me be clear: One drunk driver on the road, regardless of
gender, is too many. And to the families of people injured or
killed by female drunk drivers, statistics don't mean a damned
thing. But still, whipping up alarm over a "disturbing trend"
of women drinking more, driving drunk and taking their kids
along for the ride, based on sketchy evidence—that, even

when taken at face value, shows that fewer than 3 percent of women overall report abusing alcohol and fewer than 20 percent of DUI arrests are of women—serves no real purpose other than gender policing. Bad Mommies must be called out at every possible opportunity, reminding us all that they are *everywhere*, and the rest of us have a moral duty to save today's kids from their own selfish mothers. Women who behave "like men" must be reminded not only that this is unacceptable, but it can have deadly consequences. And we all must be reminded of what causes such reckless behavior: Women who "feel more empowered, more equal to men." Obviously, we must put a stop to *that* crap before anyone else dies. Thank god we can always find statistics to help.

6

Illegal Immigrants Make Streets and Highways Unsafe

Carolyn Cooke

Carolyn Cooke is a contributing editor to FamilySecurityMatters .org, the website for Family Security Matters, Inc., an organization dedicated to informing American citizens about issues affecting national security.

An illegal immigrant driving under the influence caused the death of an American couple, and although he was convicted in court, his illegal status and poor driving record should have been addressed long before the fatal crash. Insufficient immigration laws have failed society, and illegal immigrants account for too many drunk driving accidents.

Marine Corporal Brian Mathews was home on a three-day leave for the 2006 Thanksgiving holiday. He had finished an eight-month tour of duty in Iraq and was planning to leave the military in June, 2007. Corporal Mathews, 21 years old, had enlisted in the Marines on his 17th birthday.

Brian's mom, Trudy, had been worried about her son's decision to enlist. This trip home was a rare moment of peace for her.

"He felt on top of his world," Mrs. Mathews said. "He was real happy. Very, very happy."

Brian told his mom how Southwest Airlines had let him board first and thanked him for his service to the country

Carolyn Cooke, "Exclusive: America's Most Forgotten—Legally Licensed Illegal Alien Drunk Driver Kills Marine, Date," FamilySecurityMatters.org, November 18, 2009. Reproduced by permission.

over the intercom on the plane. He had plans to see his family and attend another friend's 21st birthday party while home.

A Fatal Accident

After finishing Thanksgiving dinner with his family, Brian was picked up by his date, Jennifer Bower, 24 years old, from Columbia, Maryland. They were on their second date, having been introduced by a couple whose wedding they attended the previous June. While Brian was stationed at Camp Pendleton they continued to keep in frequent contact.

Brian and Jennifer were waiting for the red light to change at the intersection of Route 175 and Route 108 in Jennifer's Toyota Corolla. Eduardo Morales-Soriano, an illegal alien with a blood alcohol level four times the legal limit, slammed into their car, spinning it around and crashing the windshield. Morales-Soriano stepped out of his Nissan Sentra, shaking his head and sat down on the guard rail according to witnesses. He had a valid Maryland driver's license.

Jennifer and Brian were taken to Maryland Shock Trauma Center where they died. When the Mathews arrived, Brian was on life support but an MRI showed no blood flow to the brain. He never gained consciousness and was pronounced dead on Friday morning.

Trudy Mathews recalled her son donating his organs when he went to renew his driver's license. "I asked him if he really wanted to do that, and he said, 'Sure, why wouldn't I? I don't need them and it could save people.' That's exactly what happened. His heart was matched right there at the hospital. And it's a good heart, a very good heart."

Brian M. Mathews, Corporal United States Marine Corps Iraq, was buried at Arlington National Cemetery on November 29, 2006.

Jennifer Bower and Brian Mathews shared a commitment of service to others.

Jennifer was buried on her 25th birthday. Friends gathered to "remember and celebrate" her life. Described as "infectious and outgoing", Jennifer was working on a master's degree in community counseling at Marymount University. She was also an intern at a halfway house working with addicts.

Jennifer wrote on her MySpace profile, "There is nothing better than the feeling of being able to help others."

At the sentencing hearing of Morales-Soriano the judge read a statement about Jennifer: "She had a kind heart and a great potential for helping others. We will always cherish who she is and what she brought to each of us."

Morales had been in the country illegally for a year. During this time, he had been charged with four counts related to a drunk driving arrest in Howard County.

Brian Mathews wanted to be in the armed services from the age of three, family members recalled. He began playing with GI Joe and wanted to follow in the foot steps of his father, Bill Mathews, and older brother, Kyle Mathews. Brian's father was a Marine who served in Vietnam and is a retired Navy Captain. Kyle was a Navy pilot and now flies for the Navy Reserves. His older sister Heather is Naval Criminal Intelligence Service investigator.

Childhood friends recalled Halloweens when Brian dressed in fatigues or as a secret service agent. Playing in the snow, he would ambush them "camouflaged in snowballs."

Manslaughter Charges

On May 28, 2008, Judge Louis Becker sentenced Morales-Soriano to 10 years in prison and five years probation after he pleaded guilty to two counts of automobile manslaughter, avoiding a jury trial. Morales-Soriano may be deported after he serves his sentence. The judge stated his immigration status was a factor in the sentencing.

After months of attending court hearings and rarely discussing the case publicly, the Mathews family spoke after the trial to express their frustration with the sentencing.

Trudy Mathews stated, "I am not going to get consolation from this." She said, "It is ironic, because he (Brian) fought for the system and it failed him."

Morales-Soriano's attorney, Brad Goldbloom, said after sentencing that he was surprised his client's immigration status was a factor.

Morales had been in the country illegally for a year. During this time, he had been charged with four counts related to a drunk driving arrest in Howard County. This case was dropped. Morales-Soriano was never prosecuted, nor was his license suspended.

With Thanksgiving approaching, families and friends must once again deal with the loss of these two young people who should be seated at their family tables enjoying a festive occasion if not for the failure of our federal government to uphold immigration law. An Iraqi war veteran and American hero and a lovely, dedicated young woman, both with bright futures were taken not only from their families on that Thanksgiving night, but America lost two bright stars.

7

The Issues of Immigration and Drunk Driving Should Not Be Linked

Roger Chesley

Roger Chesley is a member of the newsroom staff at the Virginian-Pilot.

While drunk driving is a serious problem, it should not be linked with immigration politics. People who try to combine the two issues abuse the current debate over immigration reform to create fear and anxiety. Illegal immigrants are no more and no less likely to drive under the influence than any other group of people. They are parents and hard workers, and should not be demonized.

It's terrible that a man awaiting a deportation ruling is suspected of killing a nun and critically injuring two others in Northern Virginia last week while driving drunk. He'd been charged at least twice earlier for drunken driving.

It's also terrible that a U.S. citizen from Virginia Beach just pleaded guilty to a drunken driving wreck in January, in which he killed a husband and wife from England; they were visiting relatives at the Beach.

Politicians and others have pointed to Carlos Martinelly Montano's case in Prince William County as a classic example of America's vulnerable borders and lax immigration laws. He should've been sent back to his native Bolivia before the crash, they fume.

Roger Chesley, "Don't Conflate the Issues of Immigration, Drunken Driving," The *Virginian-Pilot*, August 9, 2010. Reproduced by permission.

But why is there no venom about the case of Christopher Dockiewicz, who killed a couple who had been married nearly 53 years? Even though he had been speeding at 77 to 100 mph. Even though he had a blood-alcohol concentration of at least 0.13, well over the legal limit.

Double Standards Are an Outrage

People drive me nuts when they combine drunken driving incidents with the nation's immigration policy. It's as if killing someone with a car—as long as the driver is from this country—isn't worth outrage.

We pile up enough carnage from drunken driving every year in Virginia. In 2009, 316 people died and 6,256 others were injured in alcohol-related crashes; 39 of those deaths occurred in the five cities of South Hampton Roads. Statewide, more than 25,000 motorists last year were recorded with a blood-alcohol concentration of 0.08 or more.

I oppose drunken driving by anyone.

But linking those cases to immigration deficiencies is merely red meat for xenophobes [people who fear others who are different than themselves]. The same politicos and pundits never discuss the trade-offs of making the borders more secure.

Corey Stewart, a Republican, is chairman of Prince William County's Board of Supervisors. In the wake of the nun's death there, Stewart stated: "Blood is on the hands of Congress for not properly funding immigration enforcement."

He should know better. Less than a week before the wreck, *The Washington Post* reported that the Immigration and Customs Enforcement agency expects to deport about 400,000 people this fiscal year, nearly 10 percent more than the Bush administration's 2008 total and 25 percent more than in 2007. Also, the Obama administration has been auditing hundreds of businesses that have hired undocumented workers. (The president is a Democrat, and both the House and Senate have Democratic majorities.)

Real Problems Need to Be Debated

Can more be done to fix the problem of the estimated 11 million illegal immigrants in the U.S.? Yes.

Let's start with the backlog of cases.

A Syracuse University research institute this year reported that more than 228,000 deportation and asylum cases clog the system. More judges could be hired more quickly.

Can we afford to spend more money on immigration while fighting two wars, a lousy economy and high unemployment? What is the real threat from having so many illegals in this country?

We should debate these questions.

And we should keep drunks off our roads—no matter their citizenship status.

8

Intensive Treatment for Alcoholism Is Needed to Cure Repeat DUI Offenders

Jennifer McKee

Jennifer McKee is a state bureau reporter for the Billings Gazette.

Drunk driving repeat offenders are, in most cases, alcoholics who are unable to stop themselves. That is why many classes offered for DUI offenders are virtually useless and off target. Instead, intensive treatment for alcoholism is needed for drunk drivers to sober up and get their lives back on track. The costs of treatment are prohibitively expensive if offenders would have to pay out of their own pocket, and government funded treatment might prove unpopular with taxpayers. Yet while new alcohol-sensing devices might seem more cost-effective, their success remains highly doubtful.

A s a drunk, Mark Madon was extraordinarily lucky.

He drove drunk lots of times but never killed anybody. He never even injured anyone, including himself. And when he finally got popped with his fourth DUI—a felony—he was lucky enough to land a spot in Montana's lockdown alcohol treatment center at Warm Springs.

"I'm able to feel again," said Madon, 45, of Belgrade, who graduated in January from the Department of Corrections'

Jennifer McKee, "Solving the DUI Riddle," *Billings Gazette*, March 28, 2010. Reproduced by permission.

program for repeat drunken drivers, the Warm Springs Addiction Treatment and Change program, or WATCh.

Montana lawmakers on the Interim Law and Justice Committee have been studying drunken-driving issues for months, with an eye toward the 2011 Legislature, where DUI is expected to be a key issue. The group is trying to find a way to cut the number of people who drink and drive, particularly the stubborn minority who do it repeatedly.

A Complex Issue

Legislators are finding what Madon already knows: The journey to sobriety—out of that world where drunken driving routinely happens—is imperfect and complex. Parts of the current legal system simply don't work. Lawmakers heard from expert after expert, stressing the need for earlier treatment for drunken drivers, but treatment costs money and nobody seems to have any, including the state. So far, they've not proposed any concrete changes.

Part of the problem is defining the problem: Is drunken driving a drinking problem or a driving problem.

For Madon, that part is easy.

"I had a drinking problem," he said, and many chemical dependency experts agree. They say that drunken driving is not a traffic offense but a violent offense, and it shouldn't be treated like speeding, particularly in the first, second or third offenses.

But there are others who say that part of the problem does point to Montana's driving realities. Taxis and other forms of public transportation are rare, said Richard Buley, a Missoula lawyer who has defended clients charged with DUI since 1981. Most cities have intentionally zoned drinking establishments away from the neighborhoods where people live, meaning most Montanans must drive to and from a bar.

Alcohol Is an Age-Old Problem

"You've got to" drive, Buley said, adding that it is unrealistic to think Montanans are going to stop getting drunk in bars given that alcohol has been a part of human culture for thousands of years.

Dealing with the driving piece will not solve the individual problems of alcoholism, but there is some evidence that it could make the roads safer. The Testicle Festival, near Missoula, is an example, Buley said.

Held every August at Rock Creek Lodge about 15 miles out of town, the festival is a celebration of Rocky Mountain oysters—bull testicles breaded and fried—and is often heavily seasoned by booze. Buley said he used to get calls every year from festival-goers who had been arrested for DUI on their way back into town.

Many people, when drunk, wouldn't attempt something that they perceive as hard or dangerous.

Then the festival changed its policies: Once you go in, you can't come out. You have to spend the night at the nearby campground.

"So there just aren't any arrests," Buley said.

And there is something about how routine driving is that leads people to think it's safe and they can easily do it, even after a few beers, said David Carter, a deputy Yellowstone County attorney. Many people, when drunk, wouldn't attempt something that they perceive as hard or dangerous.

"Like tightrope walking," he said. But driving is something almost all Montanans do every single day; it's easy. And even drunken drivers manage to get home safely about "90 percent of the time," he said.

But when they don't get home OK, the consequences are deadly—and, sadly, preventable.

Treatment Is Better than Punishment

Madon and counselors like Mona Sumner of Billings' Rimrock Foundation treatment center or Mike Ruppert, of Helena's Boyd Andrew treatment center, say that the best way to deal with DUI on a broad scale is to treat the alcoholic behind the wheel, not try to make it more difficult or less necessary for the drunk to drive.

But Montana's current legal scheme means that for most alcoholics, effective, mandated treatment doesn't come until the fourth time they get caught. Here's why: Driving while intoxicated is a misdemeanor offense until the fourth time, when it becomes a felony.

Felons and misdemeanants move through different systems. From start to finish, felons are a state problem. They are charged in state-funded courts and punished by the state-funded Department of Corrections.

Madon said he wished he had been sent to WATCh long before his fourth DUI. But WATCh, which doesn't cost the drunk a dime, is only for felons.

Those convicted of misdemeanors, by contrast, are a local problem. If they serve any jail time, it's in a county-funded local jail, and most drunken drivers are handled by locally supported city courts.

Ruppert said drunk drivers should be screened after their first offense and those identified as addicts should get the kind of treatment they need right then.

The question is how to pay for it.

Treatment Is Expensive

Missoula City Attorney Jim Nugent said cities don't have the money to be sending hundreds of drunken drivers to the kind of effective, intense treatment that will actually work.

Another option is to make the offender pay for it. But even the cost of less expensive, outpatient meaningful treatment is still beyond the means of many people, particularly confirmed alcoholics who may already have a hard time paying their bills, Buley said.

"It sounds good in theory, as punishment, but they just can't do it," he said.

There is some alcohol education legally mandated after every DUI arrest. Those convicted of misdemeanors must attend a mandatory, self-paid alcohol education, known by the initials ACT. But according to Madon and other chemical dependency experts, those classes fail to rehabilitate addicts.

Madon took those classes three times.

"It was pretty much a big waste of everybody's time," he said.

Even now, judges may sentence someone to more intense treatment after a first DUI offense.

"But very rarely does that happen," Ruppert said. And on second offense, the law says drunken drivers "shall go" to treatment.

But the treatment they're getting "is not what they need," Ruppert said. "It needs to be intensive treatment."

There is some alcohol education legally mandated after every DUI arrest.

Intensive outpatient treatment is defined by the U.S. Department of Health and Human Services' Center for Substance Abuse Treatment as treatment with a minimum of nine hours per week. It can be during the day or evenings, and addicts usually receive both group and individual therapy.

Not every drunken driver even needs treatment. About 80 percent of people charged with drunken driving once never do it again, Ruppert said. For them, the shame, inconvenience and existing legal punishments are sufficient to keep them from re-offending.

Of course, those people are generally not alcoholics, he said.

The remaining 20 percent are the problem. And for them, treatment must come before their fourth offense if Montana wants to cut down on the number of repeat drunken drivers, Ruppert said.

Sumner, the Billings counselor, said there are ways to get at meaningful treatment more cheaply. She points to Yellowstone County's drug and DUI court as a success. Such treatment courts get alcoholics plugged into services only days after their arrest, and the treatment piece is built around the needs of the addict, meaning very few people actually need inpatient treatment.

Funding for Effective Treatment Is Scarce

Right now, that treatment—both outpatient and inpatient—is paid for either by state human services money or from federal grants. But that's because the court is a "pilot program." To expand it and make drug courts a wider part of the solution, Sumner said, would require more state money.

"It's OK to get started with grant funds," she said. But the program can't grow that way.

With Montana expecting a big budget shortfall next year, spending any new money on anything could face tough sledding in the 2011 Legislature.

Supreme Court Chief Justice Mike McGrath has proposed taking a portion of the existing alcohol tax and using that to pay for, among other things, expanding drug courts. McGrath launched a drive last month to put that idea to Montana voters next year as an initiative.

However, at least one lawmaker on the Interim Law and Justice Committee, Sen. Jon Esp, R-Big Timber, pointed out that McGrath's idea doesn't completely solve the funding challenge. Alcohol tax money currently funds other government services.

McGrath's idea would spend $10 million of it on drug and DUI courts. That's $10 million lawmakers will have to cut from somewhere else; it's not $10 million in new money.

It's not just money that's a problem, said Carter, the Billings prosecutor.

Right now, people convicted of a misdemeanor can be given a maximum 12-month sentence. That means judges have power over them only for a year. It sometimes takes longer than a year to complete treatment.

Carter proposes making a new kind of misdemeanor charge, an "aggravated misdemeanor," for certain DUIs that have all the markers of alcoholism, such as extremely high blood-alcohol levels or driving drunk with children in the car.

Under Carter's proposal, drunken drivers convicted of aggravated DUI could be on probation for longer than a year, long enough for a judge to force treatment.

New Technology Might Help

Attorney General Steve Bullock has also unveiled his 24/7 Sobriety Project, which begins on a limited scale in Lewis and Clark County in May. That program, modeled after South Dakota's successful project of the same name, makes those accused of a second DUI submit to twice-daily Breathalyzer tests, at the offenders' expense.

Offenders who live too far away from a Breathalyzer site would wear a special bracelet that monitors the alcohol content of their sweat.

Bullock said the simple strategy will help "change the behavior" of repeat drunken drivers because the consequences of drinking again are immediate: jail time.

In South Dakota, the 24/7 program has seen success: More than 99 percent of the 12,000-plus people who have been through the program pass their breath tests, and South Dakota saw the nation's biggest drop in alcohol-related fatal crashes from 2006 to 2008.

The cost is relatively cheap: About $115 a month for offenders who can use the Breathalyzer test or around $210 for the ankle bracelet, known by its acronym of SCRAM. Offenders would pay the costs. In South Dakota, the program is self-supporting, which Bullock said he expects to be the case here.

More Challenges Lie Ahead

Buley cautioned that such ankle bracelets may not be all they're cracked up to be.

"SCRAM is a fantastic piece of marketing," he said. And they're expensive.

"If people could afford that, they wouldn't be having public defenders," he said. "You're putting another burden on people. It's wear that or go to jail. It's insane."

Whatever the state does, Madon said changes need to be made. He offers his own life as proof.

Before treatment, before WATCh, before he became a felon, Madon was not just a drunken driver. He was a man whose life was coming undone.

"I was looking at my marriage failing, looking at losing everything I'd worked for," he said. "I felt pretty hopeless. The biggest thing was my drinking problem."

A construction subcontractor, Madon was able to put his job "on hold" while he attended WATCh.

"My wife and I, our relationship is a thousand times better," he said. "We are able to talk to each other without it being a screaming match. Her biggest issue was the way I drank."

Treating Drunk Drivers for Alcoholism Is Better than Jailing Them

Jay Winsten

Jay Winsten is an Associate Dean and the Frank Stanton Director of the Center for Health Communication at the Harvard School of Public Health.

Studies have shown that intensive treatment for alcoholism can reduce the number of repeat DUI offenders. Just as the concept of the designated driver—an example of searching for solutions beyond merely punitive measures—has shown that drunk driving can be reduced significantly, treatment will aid drunk drivers whom the court system has failed.

Police say that Anthony Galluccio, a Massachusetts state senator and former mayor of Cambridge, MA, was "pretty drunk" in the early hours of October 4 [2009]. Galluccio walked into Basha Café in Cambridge sometime after 2:00 am. The night manager gave him something to eat, and offered to drive him home. Galluccio accepted the ride, but was too drunk to provide accurate directions. In frustration, the night manager eventually pulled into a gas station, called 911 at 4:39 am, and told the dispatcher, according to the official police report, "that he did not let Mr. Galluccio drive his car, that he did not know where Mr. Galluccio lived, . . . that Mr. Galluccio was totally drunk." A police cruiser responded, and the two officers offered a ride home to their former mayor. Eventually they found his residence.

Jay Winsten, "Stopping Drunk Drivers," The *Huffington Post*, December 21, 2009. Reproduced by permission of the author.

Several hours later, Galluccio was back behind the wheel, and rear-ended another car at an intersection. The other driver suffered back and neck injuries, and Galluccio fled the scene. This past Friday, Galluccio pleaded guilty in Cambridge District Court to leaving the scene of a crash involving injury. The district attorney asked for six months in prison, but Galluccio received six months of home confinement, and can leave home to go to church or attend formal sessions of the Senate. He was ordered to surrender his driver's license for five years, and to submit to random alcohol testing. Galluccio apologized to the court, and issued a public statement vowing to seek treatment and remain alcohol-free.

A Continued Saga

So far, this is a "good news" story. No one was killed when Galluccio slammed into the car. And, the manager at the café deserves a medal for intervening to prevent Galluccio from driving that night. But Galluccio has two prior convictions for drunk driving (he received a pardon from former Governor William Weld for one of them), and he previously left the scene of another crash. So, this saga may not be over yet.

Studies found that millions of heavy drinkers, as well as light social drinkers, adopted the practice of choosing a designated driver.

Galluccio's story is worth re-telling because it illuminates the long road that still lies ahead to keep our roads—and ourselves—safe from drunk drivers. Tremendous progress has been made in the U.S. in reducing alcohol-related fatalities through a combination of tough laws, strict enforcement, and media campaigns, but we've been stymied when it's come to changing the behavior of hard-core, problem-drinkers and alcoholics.

This month, the Harvard School of Public Health is marking the "21st Birthday" (i.e., legal drinking age) of the National Designated Driver Campaign, which the School launched in late 1988 in partnership with leading TV networks and Hollywood studios. The campaign successfully demonstrated how a new social concept—the "designated driver"—could be rapidly introduced into American society, importing the concept from Scandinavia through mass communication and catalyzing a fundamental shift in social norms. The campaign broke new ground when TV writers agreed to depict the use of designated drivers in more than 160 prime-time episodes of programs such as Cheers, L.A. Law, and The Cosby Show. Public opinion polls found that a majority of Americans embraced the practice of choosing a designated driver, suggesting that the campaign, along with other factors, contributed to a steep decline in alcohol-related traffic fatalities.

Designated Drivers Reduce Fatalities

When we launched the campaign in late 1988, the annual number of alcohol-related traffic fatalities stood at 23,000. Today that number has been reduced to 13,000. Studies found that millions of heavy drinkers, as well as light social drinkers, adopted the practice of a designated driver. Alcoholics, however, are often in denial about their drinking problem, and cannot be reached effectively through media or law enforcement. It takes a concerted effort of interpersonal interventions, initiated by people around them, to keep these individuals off the road and get them into professional treatment programs or peer support groups such as Alcoholics Anonymous.

Our courts can lock someone up for a long time after a fatal crash. But courts alone can't prevent that crash. On the other hand, the legal system can do much more than was accomplished in Cambridge District Court in Galluccio's recent case. More than twenty years ago, in nearby Quincy District Court, now retired Chief Judge Albert Kramer pioneered an aggressive and effective approach, based on data showing that most first-offenders appearing before him were alcoholics or problem drinkers. (The explanation is that the odds of an arrest for drunk driving are quite low, which means that, on average, a driver will make many trips while intoxicated prior to getting caught.) Kramer sent first-offenders to an evaluation center, and those diagnosed as problem drinkers were sentenced to a 6-month, intensive treatment program. The bottom line: recidivism rates declined.

10

Lowering the Drinking Age Would Reduce Many Alcohol-Related Problems

John M. McCardell, Jr.

John M. McCardell, Jr. is the 16th Vice Chancellor of The University of the South and president emeritus of Middlebury College. He is also the president and founder of Choose Responsibility, a nonprofit group that raises awareness of and contributes to public debate over the age of twenty-one as legal drinking age.

Initiatives against drunk driving have lowered the rates of traffic fatalities, yet society needs to go beyond measures enacted some 30 years ago in order to further decrease the number of drunk driving accidents. The US should lower the minimum legal drinking age and license young adults for drinking, based on the model of drivers' licenses. Only if adolescents and young adults are taught to drink openly and responsibly will deadly binges and drunk driving accidents decrease. Society cannot stop young adults from experimenting with alcohol, but it can make drinking much safer.

One year ago, a group of college and university presidents and chancellors, eventually totaling 135, issued a statement that garnered national attention.

The "Amethyst Initiative" put a debate proposition before the public—"Resolved: That the 21-year-old drinking age is not working." It offered, in much the way a grand jury per-

John McCardell, Jr., "Commentary: Drinking Age of 21 Doesn't Work," CNN.com, September 16, 2009. © 2009 CNN. Reproduced by permission.

forms its duties, sufficient evidence for putting the proposition to the test. It invited informed and dispassionate public debate and committed the signatory institutions to encouraging that debate. And it called on elected officials not to continue assuming that, after 25 years, the status quo could not be challenged, even improved.

One year later, the drinking age debate continues, and new research reinforces the presidential impulse. Just this summer a study published in the *Journal of the American Academy of Child and Adolescent Psychiatry* revealed that, among college-age males, binge drinking is unchanged from its levels of 1979; that among non-college women it has increased by 2.0 percent; and that among college women it has increased by 40 percent.

Misinformation Abounds

Remarkably, the counterintuitive conclusion drawn by the investigators, and accepted uncritically by the media, including editorials in *The New York Times* and *The Washington Post* is that the study proves that raising the drinking age to 21 has been a success.

More recently, a study of binge drinking published in the *Journal of the American Medical Association* announced that "despite efforts at prevention, the prevalence of binge drinking among college students is continuing to rise, and so are the harms associated with it."

Worse still, a related study has shown that habits formed at 18 die hard: "For each year studied, a greater percentage of 21- to 24-year-olds [those who were of course once 18, 19 and 20] engaged in binge drinking and driving under the influence of alcohol."

Yet, in the face of mounting evidence that those young adults age 18 to 20 toward whom the drinking age law has been directed are routinely—indeed in life- and health-threatening ways—violating it, there remains a belief in the land that a minimum drinking age of 21 has been a "success." And elected officials are periodically reminded of a provision in the 1984 law that continues to stifle any serious public debate in our country's state legislative chambers: Any state that sets its drinking age lower than 21 forfeits 10 percent of its annual federal highway appropriation.

But it's not 1984 anymore.

It Is Time for a New Debate

This statement may seem obvious, but not necessarily. In 1984 Congress passed and the president signed the National Minimum Drinking Age Act. The Act, which raised the drinking age to 21 under threat of highway fund withholding, sought to address the problem of drunken driving fatalities. And indeed, that problem was serious.

States that lowered their ages during the 1970s and did nothing else to prepare young adults to make responsible decisions about alcohol witnessed an alarming increase in alcohol-related traffic fatalities.

It was as though the driving age were lowered but no drivers education were provided. The results were predictable.

Now, 25 years later, we are in a much different, and better, place. Thanks to the effective public advocacy of organizations like Mothers Against Drunk Driving, we are far more aware of the risks of drinking and driving. Automobiles are much safer.

Seatbelts and airbags are mandatory. The "designated driver" is now a part of our vocabulary. And more and more states are mandating ignition interlocks for first-time DUI offenders, perhaps the most effective way to get drunken drivers off the road.

And the statistics are encouraging. Alcohol-related fatalities have declined over the last 25 years. Better still, they have declined in all age groups, though the greatest number of deaths occurs at age 21, followed by 22 and 23. We are well on the way to solving a problem that vexed us 25 years ago.

Solving a New Problem

The problem today is different. The problem today is reckless, goal-oriented alcohol consumption that all too often takes place in clandestine locations, where enforcement has proven frustratingly difficult. Alcohol consumption among young adults is not taking place in public places or public view or in the presence of other adults who might help model responsible behavior. But we know it is taking place.

Of the 5,000 lives lost to alcohol each year by those under 21, more than 60 percent are lost off the roadways.

If not in public, then where? The college presidents who signed the Amethyst Initiative know where. It happens in "pre-gaming" sessions in locked dorm rooms where students take multiple shots of hard alcohol in rapid succession, before going to a social event where alcohol is not served. It happens in off-campus apartments beyond college boundaries and thus beyond the presidents' authority; and it happens in remote fields to which young adults must drive.

And the Amethyst presidents know the deadly result: Of the 5,000 lives lost to alcohol each year by those under 21, more than 60 percent are lost OFF the roadways, according to the National Institute of Alcoholism and Alcohol Abuse.

The principal problem of 2009 is not drunken driving. The principal problem of 2009 is clandestine binge drinking.

Young Adults Experience 'Prohibition'

That is why the Amethyst presidents believe a public debate is so urgent. The law does not say drink responsibly or drink in moderation. It says don't drink. To those affected by it, those who in the eyes of the law are, in every other respect legal adults, it is Prohibition. And it is incomprehensible.

The principal impediment to public debate is the 10 percent highway penalty. That penalty should be waived for those states that choose to try something different, which may turn out to be something better. But merely adjusting the age—up or down—is not really the way to make a change.

We should prepare young adults to make responsible decisions about alcohol in the same way we prepare them to operate a motor vehicle: by first educating and then licensing, and permitting them to exercise the full privileges of adulthood so long as they demonstrate their ability to observe the law.

The United States is one of only four countries—the others are Indonesia, Mongolia and Palau—with an age as high as 21.

Licensing would work like drivers education—it would involve a permit, perhaps graduated, allowing the holder the privilege of purchasing, possessing and consuming alcohol, as each state determined, so long as the holder had passed an alcohol education course and observed the alcohol laws of the issuing state.

Breeding Disrespect For The Law

Most of the rest of the world has come out in a different place on the drinking age. The United States is one of only four countries—the others are Indonesia, Mongolia and Palau—with an age as high as 21. All others either have no minimum age or have a lower age, generally 18, with some at 16.

Young adults know that. And, in their heart of hearts, they also know that a law perceived as unjust, a law routinely violated, can over time breed disrespect for law in general.

Slowly but surely we may be seeing a change in attitude. This summer, Dr. Morris Chafetz, a distinguished psychiatrist, a member of the presidential commission that recommended raising the drinking age, and the founder of the National Institute for Alcoholism and Alcohol Abuse admitted that supporting the higher drinking age is "the most regrettable decision of my entire professional career." This remarkable statement did not receive the attention it merited.

Alcohol is a reality in the lives of young adults. We can either try to change the reality—which has been our principal focus since 1984, by imposing Prohibition on young adults 18 to 20—or we can create the safest possible environment for the reality.

A drinking age minimum of 21 has not changed the reality. It's time to try something different.

It's not 1984 anymore.

11

Sobriety Checkpoints Are Profitable but Do Not Prevent Drunk Driving

Ryan Gabrielson

Ryan Gabrielson joined California Watch *in 2009 and covers public safety issues. He is the recipient of a Pulitzer Prize and was an investigative reporting fellow at University of California Berkeley.*

Sobriety checkpoints in the state of California exist officially to catch drunk drivers and make the roads safer, but more and more, these checkpoints become a lucrative side business for local communities. Instead of cracking down on DUI offenders, the police impounds cars and shares the money generated from fees and fines with towing businesses. Recently, sobriety checkpoints have come under scrutiny because they are set up mostly in Hispanic neighborhoods, targeting illegal immigrants who often don't possess the money to retrieve their cars. Legal challenges may stop the practice, but police and local authorities defend the measure as a safety precaution.

Sobriety checkpoints in California are increasingly turning into profitable operations for local police departments that are far more likely to seize cars from unlicensed motorists than catch drunken drivers.

An investigation by the Investigative Reporting Program at UC Berkeley with California Watch has found that impounds

Ryan Gabrielsen, "Car Seizures at DUI Checkpoints Prove Profitable for Cities, Raise Legal Questions," *California Watch*, a project of The Center for Investigative Reporting. February 13, 2010. Reproduced by permission.

at checkpoints in 2009 generated an estimated $40 million in towing fees and police fines—revenue that cities divide with towing firms.

A Source of Revenue

Additionally, police officers received about $30 million in overtime pay for the DUI crackdowns, funded by the California Office of Traffic Safety.

In dozens of interviews over the past three months, law enforcement officials and tow truck operators say that vehicles are predominantly taken from minority motorists—often illegal immigrants.

In the course of its examination, the Investigative Reporting Program reviewed hundreds of pages of city financial records and police reports, and analyzed data documenting the results from every checkpoint that received state funding during the past two years. Among the findings:

- Sobriety checkpoints frequently screen traffic within, or near, Hispanic neighborhoods. Cities where Hispanics represent a majority of the population are seizing cars at three times the rate of cities with small minority populations. In South Gate, a Los Angeles County city where Hispanics make up 92 percent of the population, police confiscated an average of 86 vehicles per operation last fiscal year.

- The seizures appear to defy a 2005 federal appellate court ruling that determined police cannot impound cars solely because the driver is unlicensed. In fact, police across the state have ratcheted up vehicle seizures. Last year, officers impounded more than 24,000 cars and trucks at checkpoints. That total is roughly seven times higher than the 3,200 drunken driving arrests at roadway operations. The percentage of vehicle seizures has increased 53 percent statewide compared to 2007.

- Departments frequently overstaff checkpoints with officers, all earning overtime. The Moreno Valley Police Department in Riverside County averaged 38 officers at each operation last year, six times more than federal guidelines say is required. Nearly 50 other local police and sheriff's departments averaged 20 or more officers per checkpoint—operations that averaged three DUI arrests a night.

Denial of Racial Targeting

Law enforcement officials say demographics play no role in determining where police establish checkpoints.

Indeed, the Investigative Reporting Program's analysis did not find evidence that police departments set up checkpoints to specifically target Hispanic neighborhoods. The operations typically take place on major thoroughfares near highways, and minority motorists are often caught in the checkpoints' net.

"All we're looking for is to screen for sobriety and if you have a licensed driver," said Capt. Ralph Newcomb of the Montebello Police Department. "Where you're from, what your status is, that never comes up."

Additionally, the 2005 appellate court ruling includes exceptions, allowing police to seize a vehicle driven by an unlicensed motorist when abandoning it might put the public at risk. Examples include vehicles parked on a narrow shoulder or obstructing fire lanes.

But reporters attending checkpoints in Sacramento, Hayward and Los Angeles observed officers impounding cars that appeared to pose no danger.

Reporters also noted that many of the drivers who lost their cars at these checkpoints were illegal immigrants, based on interviews with the drivers and police. They rarely challenge vehicle seizures or have the cash to recover their cars, studies and interviews show.

Many Cars Are Not Recovered

Some tow truck company officials relayed stories of immigrant mothers arriving at impound lots to remove baby car seats and children's toys before leaving the vehicle to the tow firm.

"I have to stand here for days and watch them take their whole life out of their vehicles," said Mattea Ezgar, an office manager at Terra Linda Towing in San Rafael.

This wasn't what lawmakers intended when they passed an impound law 15 years ago—the same law that the federal court has since questioned, said David Roberti, former president of the state Senate.

"When something is that successful, then maybe it's too easy to obtain an impoundment, which should usually be way more toward the exception than the rule," Roberti said.

The impound law granted police the authority to seize unlicensed drivers' cars for 30 days. The California Attorney General's Office said in a written statement that the state law is murky in terms of whether vehicles driven by unlicensed motorists can be taken at all.

Police do not typically seize the cars of motorists arrested for drunken driving, meaning the owners can retrieve their vehicles the next day, according to law enforcement officials.

The checkpoints have rocked lives of sober motorists.

To be sure, DUI checkpoints have saved countless lives on the nation's roadways and have brought thousands of drunken drivers to justice. And by inspecting driver's licenses, police catch motorists driving unlawfully, typically without insurance, and temporarily remove them from the road.

With support from groups such as Mothers Against Drunk Driving, California more than doubled its use of sobriety checkpoints the past three years.

State officials have declared that 2010 will be the "year of the checkpoint." Police are scheduling 2,500 of the operations in every region of California. Some departments have begun to broaden the definition of sobriety checkpoints to include checking for unlicensed drivers.

Checkpoint Impact Not Limited to Drunken Drivers

The checkpoints have rocked lives of sober motorists such as Luis Gomez.

In the early evening of Jan. 2 of this year, [2010] Gomez was driving his Chevy truck through downtown Los Angeles when traffic slowed to a stop.

A couple blocks from the Staples Center, orange cones narrowed Olympic Boulevard's three westbound lanes to two. Los Angeles Police Department officers, stationed beneath a freeway overpass, began questioning drivers as part of a DUI checkpoint.

Gomez, a 42-year-old construction worker, said the road-block didn't concern him. He said he doesn't drink alcohol.

But the illegal immigrant was driving without a license. Gomez received a traffic citation.

A tow truck operator took his truck.

Owners who do recover their vehicles pay between $1,000 and $4,000 in tow and storage charges and fines assessed by local governments, municipal finance records show.

Officers do not inquire about the drivers' residency status. Nor do they contact U.S. Immigration and Customs Enforcement when they suspect unlicensed motorists are in the country illegally.

Gomez said he'd try to save whatever money he could to get back his truck. The Chevy is critical for him to continue finding work at construction sites, jobs that have supported him for two decades in the United States.

"It's going to be hard, because times are hard," Gomez said.

Impounds Aid Cash-Strapped Local Governments

Cities have their own money problems.

Since 2007, the sales tax revenues of California municipalities have shrunk by $471 million, figures from the California State Board of Equalization show.

Property values have withered, too, causing financial woes at every level of government.

"If a city wants to try to raise revenue, in mostly all cases you have to go to the voters," said Daniel Carrigg, legislative director for the League of California Cities. Local governments, instead, are adding to fees for services and fines for an assortment of violations.

Local governments often charge unlicensed drivers a fine to get their vehicles released from impound—on average more than $150, finance records show. Cities, increasingly, also get a cut of the fees that tow operators charge vehicle owners, generating hundreds of thousands of dollars a year.

Some local governments ensure they get a larger share as their police departments seize more and more cars.

In Los Angeles County, the city of Montebello requires its tow operator to increase its cut of impound revenue when the police department seizes a higher volume of cars.

Tow company Helms and Hill Inc. pays Montebello $200 per tow when officers order more than 151 cars hauled away each month, the city's finance records show.

Montebello's DUI checkpoints rank among California's least effective at getting drunks off the road.

Last year, officers there failed to conduct a single field sobriety test at three of the city's five roadway operations, state records show.

Montebello collected upward of $95,000 during the last fiscal year from checkpoints, including grant money for police overtime.

The California Office of Traffic Safety, which is administered in part by officials at UC Berkeley, continues to fund Montebello's operations, providing a fresh $37,000 grant for this year.

Checkpoint Location May Influence Impounds

Most of the state's 3,200 roadblocks over the past two years occurred in or near Hispanic neighborhoods, the Investigative Reporting Program's analysis shows. Sixty-one percent of the checkpoints took place in locations with at least 31 percent Hispanic population. About 17 percent of the state's checkpoints occurred in areas with the lowest Hispanic population—under 18 percent.

Further, police impound the most cars per checkpoint in cities where Hispanics are a majority of the population, according to state traffic safety statistics and U.S. Census data.

An hour into the operation that evening, officers had yet to make a DUI arrest . . . but about a half dozen cars were impounded, leaving drivers stranded. Only one of the drivers could show he was a legal U.S. resident.

For 12 years, Francisco Ruiz has run El Potro, a Latin music nightclub, at the northeast corner of A Street and Hesperian Boulevard in Hayward. Not once had he seen a DUI checkpoint. Then, in 2009, the city's police department conducted four operations just outside his front door.

"They're not taking drunk drivers," Ruiz said as he watched cars crawl through a Dec. 18 [2009] checkpoint at the intersection. "They're taking people without a license."

Sobriety Checks Serve Hidden Agendas

An hour into the operation that evening, officers had yet to make a DUI arrest, reporters observed.

But about a half dozen cars were impounded, leaving drivers stranded. Only one of the drivers could show he was a legal U.S. resident.

The state does not consistently collect data on where local police departments set up checkpoints. A majority of California law enforcement agencies declined to release records showing which intersections they target, or what transpired at checkpoints, making it difficult to perform a statistical analysis of seizures in heavily minority communities.

But cities across the state operate checkpoints in high-minority communities, the Investigative Reporting Program found through demographic data and more than three dozen interviews with law enforcement officials at DUI crackdowns.

In the Los Angeles suburb of South Gate, Hispanics make up 92 percent of the population. The police department averaged 86 impounds each time officers shut down a road last year for a sobriety checkpoint. By comparison, they averaged a little more than four drunken driving arrests.

Checkpoints in cities where Hispanics are the largest share of the population seized 34 cars per operation, a rate three times higher than cities with the smallest Hispanic populations, the Investigative Reporting Program's analysis shows.

The checkpoint data tells a similar story in two-dozen other cities. A majority of these communities are crowded together east of Los Angeles within the Inland Empire.

The disparity between vehicles impounds and DUI arrests exist in virtually every region of California. . . .

Racial Considerations Are Being Denied

Impounds at DUI checkpoints are incidental, not intentional, law enforcement officials argue. And the operations do not target Hispanic communities, they say.

"Our checkpoints are sobriety and driver's license, but one thing we always emphasize: The reason why we're out here are drunk drivers," said Officer Don Inman, grant administrator for the Los Angeles Police Department's traffic division. "The driver's license, that's just a side issue that we deal with. We always try to make sure we pick in locations where we're going to get drunk drivers."

LAPD averaged six DUI arrests per checkpoint in 2009, state data shows, more than most California departments.

The state traffic safety agency requires that police wait until 6 p.m. to begin screening cars, though a few start earlier. The checkpoints typically last six hours over a single night.

Even still, the LAPD's driver's license impounds doubled the past two years. One operation in December netted 64 vehicle seizures and four drunken driving arrests.

One police agency, the California Highway Patrol, has far different results at its checkpoints. In 2008, state records show, the CHP arrested four intoxicated motorists for every one car that deputies seized.

The highway patrol does not charge a fee to release impounded vehicles and collects no revenue from seizures, said Sgt. Kevin Davis, who oversees checkpoints in CHP's research and planning division.

Setting up a Checkpoint

Police say they consider a number of factors when setting up a checkpoint.

Sgt. Dennis Demerjian, of the El Monte Police Department, said he typically consults his agencies' internal data to find intersections where clusters of alcohol-involved collisions have taken place.

Riverside County Sheriff's Office Deputy Jarod Howe said roadways must have heavy traffic to justify placing officers there.

A street needs to be wide enough to allow cars to pull off safely. Officers also need space to conduct field sobriety tests and question motorists without licenses.

And the area needs to accommodate the tow trucks to remove seized vehicles, Howe acknowledged.

Police and state traffic safety officials contend that impounding the cars of unlicensed drivers is, like catching drunken drivers, a critical part of making California's roads less dangerous.

"It's well known that drivers driving without licenses are frequently involved in accidents," said Sgt. Jeff Lutzinger, the head of Hayward's traffic safety division.

Research by the National Highway Traffic Safety Administration has shown that motorists driving with a suspended or revoked license cause collisions at a higher rate. These drivers are also typically uninsured.

The state's traffic safety office has declared vehicle seizures an effective way to remove risky, uninsured drivers.

"Law enforcement agencies have stated that these tools have helped decrease the number of unsafe drivers on public roads as well as reduce the number of hit-and-run traffic collisions," a 2005 report from the state agency said.

Funding For DUI Crackdowns Plays Major Role

The federal government provides the California Office of Traffic Safety about $100 million each year to promote responsible driving that reduces roadway deaths. Of that, $30 million goes into programs that fund drunken driving crackdowns, particularly checkpoints.

Police officer overtime accounts for more than 90 percent of the expense of sobriety checkpoints. Departments do not assign officers to work checkpoints during their regular shifts.

Law enforcement agencies tend to use more officers than a checkpoint requires, according to guidelines established by the National Highway Traffic Safety Administration.

Statewide, police departments on average deployed 18 officers at each checkpoint, according to state data. The federal traffic safety agency advises that police can set up DUI checkpoints with as few as six officers.

The additional dozen officers typical at a California roadway operation cost state and federal taxpayers an extra $5.5 million during the 2008–09 fiscal year, according to the Investigative Reporting Program's analysis.

The LAPD sent 35 officers, on average, to every sobriety crackdown.

At least a dozen officers spent hours sitting and chatting at an operation in early January [2010] in downtown Los Angeles. A couple of officers smoked cigars as they watched cars go through the screening.

Cities and private towing operators make tens of millions of dollars a year from checkpoints.

Officers seized 22 cars that evening and made one DUI arrest.

The state data shows that last fiscal year LAPD spent $16,200 per checkpoint, all of it on officer overtime.

Impounds a Lucrative Business For Cities, Towing Companies

Cities and private towing operators make tens of millions of dollars a year from checkpoints. This cash comes from tow fees and daily storage charges, finance records at a half dozen cities show.

If the car's owner cannot afford to recover the vehicle, then after 45 days, the tow operator can sell it to pay the bill.

Cities are also increasingly charging franchise fees to tow operators.

The fees give cities a cut of the more lucrative side of towing, the long-term storage costs from 30-day impounds.

In early 2007, El Monte's top officials went shopping for new tow contracts.

The suburb, east of Los Angeles, had called on tow operators to remove almost 5,000 cars a year from its streets, El Monte Police Chief Ken Weldon explained in a memo to the city manager.

The operators hauled the cars at no cost to El Monte; however the chief found the city was denying itself a source of cash.

"A survey of surrounding agencies revealed that many agencies are recovering costs by collecting a 'franchise fee' from the tow company," Weldon, now retired, wrote.

On average, nearby cities charged tow operators $50 for every car the police department ordered towed or impounded. Weldon calculated the fee would provide El Monte $241,600 a year.

The city wrote the fees into its new contracts with Albert's Towing and Freddie Mac's Towing.

During holiday checkpoints last fiscal year, El Monte police seized 680 cars for driver's license violations, state data shows.

Each of the impounds was worth at least $2,035 in tow charges and fees, according to city financial records. El Monte received at least $164,000 from the vehicle seizures.

The city's tow operators likely collected about $1.2 million from the seizures. That figure might have been higher or lower, depending on how many car owners retrieved their vehicles and what price the companies got for the remaining impounded cars.

Owners abandon their cars at tow lots roughly 70 percent of the time, said Perry Shusta, owner of Arrowhead Towing in Antioch and vice president of the California Tow Truck Association.

Tow operators provide communities a kind of garbage service, removing junk cars that don't operate and are worth only the value of their metal frame.

DUI checkpoints catch a higher quality of vehicle, Shusta said. "The good cars are how we afford to get rid of all the cities' junk."

Impounds Spur Search and Seizure Concerns

The Fourth Amendment specifically restricts law enforcement's authority to seize private property without a court order.

"It is assumed under the law that the taking of personal property without a warrant is unconstitutional," said Martin J. Mayer, a founding partner in the Fullerton law firm Jones & Mayer, which represents numerous police agencies.

The law protects everyone within the United States, regardless of whether they are in the country illegally.

California police have seized the cars of unlicensed drivers for 15 years under the state law that allows such vehicles to be impounded for 30 days.

But in 2005, the Ninth U.S. Circuit Court of Appeals ruled in an Oregon case that law enforcement can't impound a vehicle if the only offense is unlicensed driving.

One exception is called the "community caretaker" doctrine, which permits police to impound a car if it poses a threat to public safety, is parked illegally or would be vandalized imminently if left in place.

The ruling dramatically altered the law regarding vehicle impounds. In response, the Legislative Counsel of California in 2007 called into question the legality of the state's impound procedures.

"If a peace officer lawfully stops a motor vehicle on the highway and the driver of the motor vehicle is an unlicensed driver, that alone is not sufficient justification for the peace officer to cause the impoundment of the motor vehicle," Legislative Counsel Diane F. Boyer-Vine, who advises state lawmakers, wrote in a response to Sen. Gilbert A. Cedillo, D-Los Angeles. The legislative counsel has no authority over police departments.

Legal Challenges

A lawsuit challenging the constitutionality of California's 30-day impound law is awaiting oral arguments before the Ninth Circuit Court of Appeals later this year [2010]. The state and several cities that are defendants in the case argue that impounds are penalties for a criminal offense, and therefore car owners are not subject to Fourth Amendment protection.

Most California law enforcement agencies continue to seize vehicles based on driver's license violations alone.

Reporters with the Investigative Reporting Program observed police at checkpoints in three different cities impound cars after the vehicles had been moved out of harm's way and parked legally.

Mayer represents the California Peace Officers Association and also alerted law enforcement that the federal ruling prohibited the state's police from seizing cars solely on the charge of unlicensed driving.

The attorney said he was startled by his clients' angry response to his memo explaining the appeals court case.

"I never expected the volume of e-mails, phone calls and death threats all from law enforcement, especially motor officers," Mayer said. "I'm being flippant you understand. They wanted to kill me though because I'm interfering with a process they've been doing for years."

Former state Sen. Roberti, then chairman of the Senate's Judiciary Committee, said he and his fellow lawmakers did not consider how the 1995 impound law might impact unlicensed drivers.

"It's turned out to be a far more vigorous enforcement than any of us would have dreamed of at the time," he said.

12

Higher Alcohol Taxes Can Help Prevent Drunk Driving Fatalities

Jessie Schiewe

Jessie Schiewe is a science and health writer at the Los Angeles Times.

Raising alcohol taxes might yet be the best way to bring down the number of drunk driving accidents. Statistics show that there is a correlation between tax rates and traffic fatalities, and while the measure might not be popular, it could prove the cheapest and most effective way to keep drivers safe.

People love to complain about "sin taxes" on unhealthy or socially undesirable foods and beverages. We know many of you think the government has better things to do than police what you put into your mouth. But have you ever stopped to consider how these taxes can help us?

Higher Taxes Might Save Lives

Take the case of excise taxes on alcohol. Raising their price might make it financially difficult for you to host a kegger every weekend, but it also might save your life, says a recent study published online by the journal Alcoholism: *Clinical and Experimental Research.*

Going out for chocolate martinis may be fun, but "excessive alcohol consumption is the third leading preventable cause of death" in the United States, according to the study. The National Institute on Alcohol Abuse and Alcoholism says the tab for the ill effects of excessive drinking topped $185 billion in 2006.

In Florida, excise taxes for alcohol haven't been changed since 1983. Back then, a charge of 48 cents per gallon of beer was meaningful; now it's the spare change you could find at the bottom of your purse. By the same token, the $2.25 excise tax per gallon of wine and $6.50 per gallon of distilled spirits don't pack the same financial punch that they did 27 years ago.

Adjusting those taxes to account for the inflation that has taken place since Ronald Reagan's first term in the White House would not only make alcohol more expensive; it would also prevent between 600 and 800 deaths per year, according to the July 23 study by researchers from the University of Florida College of Medicine in Gainesville.

Statistics Draw a Compelling Picture

That calculation is based on data compiled by the National Center for Health Statistics, part of the Centers for Disease Control and Prevention. The database includes information on every reported death in the country, including its cause. The researchers were able to find the number of alcohol-related deaths in Florida for each month between 1969 and 2005. (These were defined as deaths from diseases in which alcohol was at least 35% to blame, including cirrhosis, alcoholic liver disease, and acute alcohol poisoning.) Then they compared those figures to the financial burden imposed by the alcohol excise taxes, which changed each month due to legislation or the effects of inflation.

In a nutshell, they found that when the tax got more expensive (due to laws passed in 1977 and 1983), the number of deaths fell. When the tax got cheaper (due to inflation), the number of deaths rose. Overall, they calculated that each $1-per-gallon increase in the alcohol tax translated into 69 fewer deaths per month.

As a result, lead author Mildred Maldonado-Molina says Floridians would benefit by bringing the state's alcohol tax into the 21st century. Factoring in the impact of inflation would boost the beer tax to $1.05 per gallon in today's dollars (or 59 cents per six-pack), the wine tax to $4.93 per gallon (about $1 per bottle), and the distilled spirits tax all the way up to $14.24 per gallon.

Drunk Driving Fatalities Might Also Be Reduced

The researchers focused on how taxes could avert deaths due to alcohol-related diseases because that question has not been addressed in many studies, Maldonado-Molina said. But higher taxes would actually save even more lives because any impediment to drinking would also reduce the number of drunk-driving accidents and violent crimes fueled by alcohol, the researchers concluded.

"The total number of deaths averted by increased alcohol taxes is much higher than the numbers reported here," they wrote.

13

Better Mass Transit Will Reduce Drunk Driving

Warren Redlich

Warren Redlich is a lawyer, entrepreneur, and politician who lives in Albany, New York.

US citizens, especially those living in rural and suburban areas, have to rely on cars for transportation, to get to and from work, drive to restaurants, and go to grocery stores. Because of this, drunk driving laws and initiatives have failed to keep DUI offenders off the road. Instead of punishing drunk drivers harshly and creating massive costs for taxpayers, society should invest in mass transit systems. Not only will buses and trains reduce traffic congestion, they will also allow citizens to have a drink and get home safely.

Drunk driving has been a hot topic in politics for the last couple of decades. Under pressure from groups like Mothers Against Drunk Driving (MADD), criminal prosecution of DUI cases has grown harsher. DUI enforcement is expensive. Mass transit would be far more effective at reducing drunk driving and provides a variety of other benefits.

Recent years have seen some high-profile DUI cases, including Congressman Vito Fossella's arrest in Virginia, and Paris Hilton's jail visit in Los Angeles. The blood-alcohol content [BAC] threshold has gone from 0.10 to 0.08, and in many states a new offense has been added for high BACs, such as

Aggravated DWI in New York and Extreme DUI in Arizona. Plea bargaining restrictions have also gotten more stringent. On top of all that, governments spend significant money advertising the criminal consequences of drunk driving.

Fines and Jail Terms Are Not Working

The truth is that criminal enforcement does not work adequately as a deterrent. Many people continue drinking and driving. Humans have had problems with alcohol for thousands of years. Combine that with the fact that alternatives to driving are inadequate in most of the US, and it's not surprising that the problem has not gone away.

As a nation we spend billions on DWI enforcement. This includes police salaries and equipment, prosecutors, court staff, jails, probation officers and more. Those billions would be better spent on increased mass transit, which would provide a genuine alternative to driving.

Mass transit has many other benefits. It doesn't just reduce drunk driving deaths, but all kinds of traffic accidents.

I lived in Hiroshima in the mid-1990s. There is a section of the city named Nagarekawa. It is home to thousands of bars but has very little parking available. In the US, many municipalities require bars to have ample parking for customers. Nagarekawa has numerous mass transit options nearby, including a trolley car, bus lines, and a train station. Japan's mass transit system is so thorough I lived well without owning a car. I don't recall ever hearing about a drunk driving problem there. Statistics indicate less than 1000 drunk driving deaths a year there, versus nearly 15,000 in the US. With a bit less than half the US population, the per capita drunk driving death rate in Japan is in the ballpark of one-tenth of ours.

Mass Transit Would Save Lives

Imagine living in a medium-sized metropolitan area. Picture a night-life district with a variety of bars and other entertainment options. How are people who go to these bars going to get home?

Now imagine that there are multiple transit options in this location reaching within a mile or so of 90% of the residents, and within a half-mile of 50% of the residents. Of course this will not take all drunk drivers off the road. If it takes only 25% of them off the road it will do more to reduce drunk driving deaths than what we're doing now.

Of course, mass transit has many other benefits. It doesn't just reduce drunk driving deaths, but all kinds of traffic accidents. It also helps the economy and reduces consumption of fossil fuels. A well-designed system changes growth patterns, reducing sprawl as the population spreads along the rails more than the roads.

So what's it going to be America—more rails or more jails? Next time you hear a politician talk about being tough on drunk driving, tell them you want mass transit.

Organizations to Contact

The editors have compiled the following list of organizations concerned with the issues debated in this book. The descriptions are derived from materials provided by the organizations. All have publications or information available for interested readers. The list was compiled on the date of publication of the present volume; names, addresses, phone and fax numbers, and e-mail and Internet addresses may change. Be aware that many organizations take several weeks or longer to respond to inquiries, so allow as much time as possible.

AAA Foundation
607 14th Street NW, Suite 201, Washington, DC   20005
(202) 638-5944 • fax: (202) 638-5943
website: www.aaafoundation.org/home

The AAA Foundation for Traffic Safety is dedicated to saving lives and reducing injuries by preventing traffic crashes. It is a not-for-profit, publicly-supported charitable educational and research organization and provides newsletters and annual reports on its website.

Al-Anon Family Group Headquarters
1600 Corporate Landing Pkwy., Virginia Beach, VA   23454
(757) 563-1600 • fax: (757) 563-1655
website: www.al-anon.alateen.org

Al-Anon is a fellowship of men, women, and children whose lives have been affected by an alcoholic family member or friend. Al-Anon Family Group Headquarters provides information on its local chapters and on its affiliated organization, Alateen. Its publications include the monthly magazine the *Forum*, the semiannual *Al-Anon Speaks Out*, the bi-monthly *Alateen Talk*, and several books, including *How Al-Anon Works, Path to Recovery Steps, Traditions, and Concepts*, and *Courage to Be Me: Living with Alcoholism*.

Alcoholics Anonymous (AA)

General Service Office, New York, NY   10163
(212) 870-3400 • fax: (212) 870-3003
website: www.aa.org

Alcoholics Anonymous is an international fellowship of people who are recovering from alcoholism. Because AA's primary goal is to help alcoholics remain sober, it does not sponsor research or engage in education about alcoholism. AA does, however, publish a catalog of literature concerning the organization as well as several pamphlets, including *Is AA for You? Young People and AA*, and *A Brief Guide to Alcoholics Anonymous*.

American Driver & Traffic Safety Association

Highway Safety Services, LLC, Indiana, PA   15701
(724) 801-8246 • fax: (724) 349-5042
website: www.adtsea.org

The American Driver and Traffic Safety Education Association (ADTSEA) is the professional association representing traffic safety educators throughout the United States and abroad. Research articles on drunk driving and other traffic safety concerns can be accessed online.

Distilled Spirits Council of the United States (DISCUS)

1250 I St. NW, Suite 900, Washington, DC   20005
(202) 628-3544
website: www.discus.org

The Distilled Spirits Council of the United States is the national trade association representing producers and marketers of distilled spirits in the United States. It seeks to ensure the responsible advertising and marketing of distilled spirits to adult consumers and to prevent such advertising and marketing from targeting individuals below the legal purchasing age. DISCUS publishes fact sheets, the periodic newsletter *News Release*, and several pamphlets, including the *Drunk Driving Prevention Act*.

International Center for Alcohol Policies (ICAP)
1519 New Hampshire Ave. NW, Washington, DC   20036
(202) 986-1159 • fax: (202) 986-2080
website: www.icap.org

The International Center for Alcohol Policies is a nonprofit organization dedicated to helping reduce the abuse of alcohol worldwide and to promote understanding of the role of alcohol in society through dialogue and partnerships involving the beverage industry, the public health community, and others interested in alcohol policy. ICAP is supported by eleven major international beverage alcohol companies. ICAP publishes reports on pertinent issues such as *Safe Alcohol Consumption, The Limits of Binge Drinking, Health Warning Labels, Drinking Age Limits, What Is a "Standard Drink"?, Government Policies on Alcohol and Pregnancy, Estimating Costs Associated with Alcohol Abuse,* and *Who are the Abstainers?*

Mothers Against Drunk Driving (MADD)
511 E. John Carpenter Fwy., No. 700, Irving, TX   75062
(800) GET-MADD • fax: (972) 869-2206
e-mail: info@madd.org
website: www.madd.org

Mothers Against Drunk Driving seeks to act as the voice of victims of drunk driving accidents by speaking on their behalf to communities, businesses, and educational groups, and by providing materials for use in medical facilities and health and driver education programs. MADD publishes the biannual *MADDvocate for Victims Magazine* and the newsletter *MADD in Action* as well as a variety of brochures and other materials on drunk driving.

National Council on Alcoholism and Drug Dependence (NCADD)
12 W. 21st St., New York, NY   10010
(212) 206-6770 • fax: (212) 645-1690
website: www.ncadd.org

NCADD is a volunteer health organization that helps individuals overcome addictions, advises the federal government on drug and alcohol policies, and develops substance abuse prevention and education programs for youth. It publishes fact sheets, such as *Youth and Alcohol*, and pamphlets, such as *Who's Got the Power? You . . . or Drugs?*

National Highway Traffic Safety Administration (NHTSA) Impaired Driving Division

1200 New Jersey Avenue, SE, Washington, DC   20590
1-888-327-4236
website: www.nhtsa.org

The National Highway Traffic Safety Administration (NHTSA), under the US Department of Transportation, was established by the Highway Safety Act of 1970. The agency is committed to achieving the highest standards of excellence in motor vehicle and highway safety, and works to help prevent crashes and their attendant costs, both human and financial. Reports and articles are published online.

National Institute on Alcoholism and Alcohol Abuse (NIAAA)

6000 Executive Blvd., Wilco Building
Bethesda, MD   20892-7003
website: www.niaaa.nih.gov

The National Institute on Alcoholism and Alcohol Abuse is one of the eighteen institutes that comprise the National Institutes of Health. NIAAA provides leadership in the national effort to reduce alcohol-related problems. NIAAA is an excellent source of information and publishes the quarterly bulletin, *Alcohol Alert*; a quarterly scientific journal, *Alcohol Research and Health*; and many pamphlets, brochures, and posters dealing with alcohol abuse and alcoholism. All of these publications, including NIAAA's congressional testimony, are available online.

Office for Substance Abuse Prevention (OSAP)
P.O. Box 2345, Rockville, MD   20847-2345
(800) 729-6686
website: www.health.org

OSAP leads US government efforts to prevent alcoholism and other drug problems among Americans. Through the NCADI, OSAP provides the public with a wide variety of information on alcoholism and other addictions. Its publications include the bi-monthly *Prevention Pipeline*, the fact sheet *Alcohol Alert*, monographs such as "Social Marketing/Media Advocacy" and "Advertising and Alcohol," brochures, pamphlets, videotapes, and posters. Publications in Spanish are also available.

Research Society on Alcoholism (RSA)
4314 Medical Pkwy., Suite 12, Austin, TX   78756
(512) 454-0022 • fax: (512) 454-0812
e-mail: debbyrsa@bga.com
website: www.rsoa.org

The RSA provides a forum for researches who share common interests in alcoholism. The society's purpose is to promote research on the prevention and treatment of alcoholism. It publishes the journal *Alcoholism: Clinical and Experimental Research* nine times a year as well as the book series Recent Advances in Alcoholism.

Bibliography

Books

A.J. Adams — *Undrunk: A Skeptic's Guide to AA.* Center City, MN: Hazelden Publishing, 2009.

Thomas Babor — *Alcohol: No Ordinary Commodity: Research and Public Policy.* New York, NY: Oxford University Press, 2010.

Douglas Beirness, Andrew Clayton, and Ward Vanlaar — *An Investigation of the Usefulness, the Acceptability and Impact on Lifestyle of Alcohol Ignition Interlocks in Drink-driving Offenders Usability of Alcolocks.* London, UK: Department for Transport, 2008.

Sarah Allen Benton — *Understanding the High-Functioning Alcoholic: Breaking the Cycle and Finding Hope.* New York, NY: Rowman & Littlefield Publishers, 2010.

Dennis Bjorklund — *Drunk Driving/DUI: A Survival Guide for Motorists.* Coralville, IA: Praetorian Publishers, 2008.

David Brown — *Drunk Driving: Athlete Career Killer: Say NO! to Drinking and Driving.* Parkway Press, July 6, 2010.

Steve Fox, Paul Armentano, Mason Tvert and Norm Stamper — *Marijuana Is Safer: So Why Are We Driving People to Drink?* White River Junction, VT: Chelsea Green Publishing, 2009.

Esther Gwinnell and Christine Adamec — *The Encyclopedia of Addictions and Addictive Behaviors.* New York: Facts on File, 2006.

Jack Hedblom and Paul McHugh — *Last Call: Alcoholism and Recovery.* Baltimore, MD: The Johns Hopkins University Press, 2007.

David Jolly — *DUI/DWI: The History of Driving Under the Influence.* Outskirts Press, 2009.

Steven Karch — *Forensic Issues in Alcohol Testing.* Boca Raton, FL: CRC Press, 2007.

John A. Lewis — *A Zero-tolerance Juvenile Alcohol Law: Why Legislation Won't Work.* El Paso, TX: LFB Scholarly Publishing, 2009.

Bob Mitchell — *Drunk Driving and Why The Carnage Continues.* Xlibris Corporation, 2010.

National Center on Addiction and Substance Abuse at Columbia University — *Women Under the Influence.* Baltimore, Md: Johns Hopkins University Press, 2006.

Elke Raes, T. Van den Neste and A. G. Verstraete — *Drug Use, Impaired Driving and Traffic Accidents.* Luxemburg: Office for Official Publications of the European Monitoring Centre for Drugs and Drug Addiction, 2008.

Lawrence E. Taylor and Steven Oberman	*Drunk Driving Defense*, Seventh Edition. Frederick, MD: Aspen Publishers, June 2010.
Doug Thorburn	*Alcoholism Myths and Realities: Removing the Stigma of Society's Most Destructive Disease.* Newport Beach, CA: Galt Publishing, 2005.
Rin Yoshida	Trends in Alcohol Abuse and Alcoholism Research. New York: Nova Science, 2007.

Periodicals

Jennifer Butters, et al.	"Illicit Drug Use, Alcohol Use and Problem Drinking Among Infrequent and Frequent Road Ragers," *Drug and Alcohol Dependence*, 2005.
Polly Curtis	"Alcohol at Home Can Cut Teenage Binge Drinking, Study Says," *Society-Guardian* (U.K.), May 11, 2007.
Mark Denney	"Officer Education, the Weapon against Impaired Driving," *Law & Order*, October 2008.
Janet Dewey-Kollen	"New Mexico on the Road to Reducing Drunk Driving," *Law & Order*, September 2008.
Janet Dewey-Kollen	"A Nation without Drunk Driving," *Law & Order*, April 2007.
Honolulu Star Bulletin	"Aim Anti-DUI Efforts at Average People," January 16, 2006.

Iowa State Daily	"Let Two Lost Lives Change Our View of Drunk Driving," February 15, 2006.
Elizabeth Kellar	"Ethics Inquiries: Drinking and Driving," *Public Management*, July 2008.
R. Cort Kirkwood	"Roadkillers: Unlicensed, Drunk-Driving Illegal Aliens Are Killing Americans and Each Other, by the Carload," *The New American*, April 2, 2007.
Robert Mann et al.	"Drinking-Driving Fatalities and Consumption of Beer, Wine and Spirits," *Drug and Alcohol Review*, 2006.
Jeanne Mejeur	"Ignition Interlocks Turn the Key and Blow: Can Technology Stop Drunk Driving?" *State Legislatures*, December 2007.
Moises Naim	"Mixed Metaphors: Why the Wars on Cancer, Poverty, Drugs, Terror, Drunk Driving, Teen Pregnancy, and Other Ills Can't Be Won," *Foreign Policy*, March 2010.
Iain O'Neil	"Teenagers Who Drink With Their Parents Are Less Likely to Binge Drink, According to a Study of 10,000 Children," *Morning Advertiser* (U.K.), May 11, 2007.

Anne Teigen and
Melissa Savage
"Last Call: Lawmakers Hope New Technology Could Mean the End to Drunken Driving," *State Legislatures*, December 2009.

USA Today
"Our View on Highway Safety: Stall Drunk Drivers," December 28, 2006.

Alexander
Wagenaar, et al.
"Effects of Legal BAC Limits on Fatal Crash Involvement: Analyses of 28 States from 1976 through 2002," *Journal of Safety Research*, 2007.

Western Mail
"End Drink-Drive Law Confusion by Opting for Zero Alcohol before Getting Behind the Wheel, Urge Campaigners; 'Drunk-Driver Took Our Son and Ruined Our Lives,'"(Cardiff, Wales), June 17, 2010.

William White
and David L.
Gasperin
"The 'Hard Core Drinking Driver': Identification, Treatment and Community Management," *Alcoholism Treatment Quarterly*, 2007.

Kurt Williamsen
"Drunk and Dumb," *The New American*, October 27, 2008.

Andrew
Woodcock
"Alcohol at Home Could Help Cut Teenage Binge Drinking," *The Scotsman* (U.K.), May 12, 2007.

Index

CPSIA information can be obtained
at www.ICGtesting.com
Printed in the USA
FFOW02n0435250714
6524FF